LEAVING THE LAND
OF NUMB

A JOURNEY TO CONNECT MY EMOTIONAL
AND SPIRITUAL LIVES

DON FOLLIS

Mountain Ash

Press

Cover Design by John Ciciora

ISBN: 9781952430725

Printed in the United States of America

AUTHOR'S NOTE

The conversations in this book are written from my best recollection of the essence, meaning and sentiment of what was said. The incidents and the people are real. Some people I have referred to without mentioning their actual names. Memory is complicated. The interpretation of events is mine alone.

For Darylee

CONTENTS

INTRODUCTION

When I was a boy in northwestern Kansas, I didn't know anything about the *Land of Numb*, even though I lived smack dab in the middle of it. In that land, everyone is *Just Fine*— families, teachers, coaches, merchants, nurses, farmers, pastors, dogs, cats. I soon knew all the lines common in that land.

"I'm Just Fine."

"It's just one of those things."

"It will all work out. It always does."

"It could have been worse."

"Just work harder."

"A lot of people have it worse than you."

"You're just going to have to get over it."

"Dry those tears up or I'll give you something to cry about."

"Put a smile on your face. You're just as happy as you want to be."

To be clear, we said all those lines with our arms crossed. And you had better believe it, my arms were crossed, and I was *Just*

Fine. I dried up those tears, because "Big boys don't cry." Of course, no one taught me any of those responses. You can't teach them—they are caught, not taught. For much of my life I have been *Just Fine.* After high school I left Colby, Kansas, and the High Plains. But it took a lot longer to leave the emotional *Land of Numb.* Occasionally, I still make a U-turn and visit the place. I've done it so many times, sometimes I don't even realize I have.

But I am happy to report that I don't live in that land anymore. I lived there well into adulthood, but for the last 25 years I have worked hard to stay out of the *Land of Numb,* doing my best to feel the full weight of painful and positive emotions that life throws at me every single day. Our emotional and spiritual lives are closely connected—way more than I ever would have ever imagined when I was growing up. And so, no, I am not *Just Fine.* Not any longer. Truthfully, no one ever is. True hope never emerges from being *Just Fine.* Hope understands that "the whole creation has been groaning as in the pains of childbirth right up to the present time." (Romans 8:22). The apostle Paul understood the connection between our emotional and spiritual lives when he wrote, "We ... glory in our sufferings, because we know that suffering produces perseverance; perseverance, character, and character, hope. And hope does not put us to shame, because God's love has been poured out into our hearts through the Holy Spirit, who has been given to us." (Romans 5:3-5). I try to live like that. It's the only way for me to be fully present in this one incredible life I have been given. It's the only way to have any lasting hope.

Philosopher Douglas Groothuis says, "Hope is a discipline that can be cultivated and even celebrated. I take it that hope ... if hard won, both consoles and inspires." When real hope does that, our soul can be at peace. In 2023, I completed 45 years of vocational ministry—25 years in campus ministry at the University of Illinois in Urbana-Champaign, seven years on a pastoral team in a large Vineyard church and 13 years directing a nonprofit counseling and mentoring ministry for pastors, helping them connect their emotional and spiritual lives.

As a young man, I got derailed in my desire to be a pastor, being married at age 18 and divorced at age 19. I didn't know that in my denomination, divorce would brand me unfit to be a pastor. Ashamed and puzzled, I reverted to being *Just Fine*, figuring it would somehow all work out in the *Land of Numb*. That is, until it no longer did. Ultimately, I came to recognize that my teenage divorce and rejection by the church because of that divorce, bound me in chains from which I could not get loose. Well, at least for a long time. Finally, I did get free, and that is the main reason I am so committed to helping others connect their emotional and spiritual lives.

For decades, Jennifer, my wife, has been my partner in this journey. Without her, I don't know that I ever would have left the *Land of Numb*. We got married July 8, 1978, in Phoenix, four years after my divorce. From the day I met Jennifer I knew that she was not from the *Land of Numb*. She can't stand the place, and she refuses to go there with me. From day one Jennifer amazed me at how she could name whatever emotion she felt. She still can. Not I. Though this old rat has come a long way, I still carry around a sheet with hundreds of emotions to help me if I need it. Sometimes I still pull it out and add a new emotion.

Mine has been a long trek. Some days I take three steps forward, and two steps back. There are a few days when Jennifer says, "Where are you, today, Don?" Back in the *Land of Numb* apparently. Thank goodness I no longer reside there permanently. Not only does Jennifer disdain that land, she pushes me to stay as far away from it as possible, challenging me to be honest, present, and feel the full weight of my emotions, whether they be painful or positive. When I lie on the couch, rest my head in her lap and hear her say, "Thank you for really being here today," I know that it does not get any better than that. If you were raised in the *Land of Numb* as I was, I am proof that you do not have to live there forever. Most days when I look into the rearview mirror, its borders are far in the distance.

I believe Jesus fully linked his emotional and spiritual lives. That's how I try to live. There's not one thing numb or *Just Fine* about Jesus. This book is part of the story of how I came to be more fully alive and present, more fully human, and more the man God created me to be.

PART ONE
WELCOME TO THE LAND OF NUMB

1

THE DRIVE

I pulled into my parents' driveway about 7 p.m. on June 21, 1974. It was the longest day of the year and the sun was still high in the western sky above Colby, Kansas. It was also the longest day of my 19-year-old life. I was full of dread and fear. I had driven 285 miles from Manhattan, Kansas, where I was cleaning and painting dorm rooms for a little school called Manhattan Christian College. I had just finished my freshman year at Kansas State University, also in Manhattan, with its limestone buildings and redbud trees. I had left for college as a newly married, idealistic 18-year-old. Now I was returning to Colby brokenhearted, on the verge of divorce, and full of self-loathing. I hadn't told my parents why I was coming back for the weekend. I called only the day before and told Mom to expect me about 7. I didn't want to tell them more, didn't want advice, and didn't want them offering to help.

I entered the kitchen door, dropped my duffel bag next to the table, hugged Mom and sat down to a warm plate of food. Mom and Dad sat across from me, watching me eat. I had been back briefly a month earlier to borrow a car. Only ten months earlier, I had driven off all smiles in a brand-new Buick LeSabre with my 19-year-old high school sweetheart at my side. The Buick was maroon with a white vinyl top, a wedding gift from her parents. Though happy, I felt sheepish and embarrassed in that new car. I never could have bought one like it myself, despite having worked 72 hours a week all summer at the Texaco station by the interstate highway. The car was a symbol to me that I wasn't ready to provide for a wife. Now the marriage was falling apart and I had returned to northwestern Kansas for the weekend, hoping I could talk my wife out of divorcing me.

"What do you think is next?" Mom asked.

"I have no idea. Stay in college, I guess. See what happens. Don't worry. I'll be *Just Fine*." In the home where I was raised with four other siblings, everyone always was *Just Fine*. The three of us around the table that night knew exactly what those words meant: "It will all work out. It always does." Even though it often didn't.

My plan for the next day was to leave the house early and drive, uninvited, to the farm of my wife's parents, hoping for the chance to talk with her, hoping to be given the chance to revive the marriage. At the end of the semester, my wife left the apartment we rented in the married student housing complex at K-State. She moved back home to spend the summer with her parents. Most of the furniture and the new car went with her.

After I finished my late supper, I picked up my bag, walked downstairs and greeted my Grandma Jennings in her basement apartment. She had lived with us since my Grandpa Jennings died in 1964. My brother Bob's and my bedroom was next to hers. She hugged me and said she was praying for me. While I was growing up, night after night I lay on Grandma's couch and watched television with her—*The Carol Burnett Show, Then*

Came Bronson, Bonanza (Grandma's favorite), *Gunsmoke* (a very close second), *Hawaii 5-0, I Dream of Jeannie* and *The Lawrence Welk Show*. Next to her recliner was a stack of *Capper's Weekly* newspapers. The newspaper was delivered to her through the mail and featured the latest farm news, conservative political views, recipes and jokes. Grandma devoured it every week. She didn't ask me why I had come home, about what had happened in the marriage or what I planned to do next. She just hugged me, and said, "It's going to be okay." As she kissed me on the cheek, I remembered exactly where she sat in the church the day I was married 10 months earlier. The blue dress she wore nearly matched my blue tuxedo.

Lying in bed that night, I prayed that the next morning my wife's dad would be out in his farmyard when I drove up the lane. The farm was 15 miles northwest of town. It was summer, when farmers would be out early working in their fields. I knew the likelihood of his hanging out in the farmyard, even at 7 a.m., was nearly zero. Still, I felt compelled to try. I had thought about leaving my wife's dad out of the equation altogether. I could just walk up to the door, knock and hope my wife might answer and invite me in. After all, we were still married. But the more I thought about it, the more it felt to me like she never really had left her parents. Even the thought of driving out to the farm the next morning made me feel like a stranger. I decided the only possible way for me to reconnect with my wife, if at all, was through her dad. The farmer was in charge of his kingdom and that's where his youngest daughter was living for the summer. If there was going to be any connection to my wife, it started with him.

On August 4, 1973, when I was 18 and she was barely 19, the farmer had given me his youngest daughter's hand in marriage. He was a likeable man, hard-working, a real leader. I admired his ability to run a big farm operation. But now I was nervous. I had driven across Kansas, hoping for a chance to talk with my wife, maybe even reconcile. Even with all the shame and confusion I felt, this unannounced trip seemed like the right thing to do. I felt I could not live with my conscience if I didn't at least try to salvage my marriage. There was no Plan B.

After tossing and turning most of the night in my old bed, I was up before 6 a.m. By 6:30, I was ready to head out the door. While I laced up my Converse tennis shoes, Dad and Mom sat at the table drinking coffee. The evening before they had asked nothing about what I was planning to do that Saturday. They finally addressed the elephant in the room. "So, what brings you back?"

"There are some people I want to see," I said, equivocating. Under any other circumstances, I would have told them the truth straight up. I added, "I just need to leave it at that." My answer could not have made that conversation more awkward. And besides, I'm sure they knew what I was up to, even though they didn't know the specifics. But this was new turf for them, and for me. None of us knew what was next, or how to proceed. Having a teenage son married and separated in less than a year was something that neither Dad, then 45, nor Mom, 41, had expected. Thankfully, that morning they didn't push me for any more details. They just let it be what it was—awkward. Dad and Mom liked my wife and had from the time we started dating when I was a junior in high school and she was a senior. As I headed out the door that Saturday morning, as he always did, Dad merely said, "Have a good day, son."

"Thanks, Dad. I'll be back." I hopped into the olive Buick Skylark Dad had let me borrow for the summer and pulled out onto Third Street. Three blocks west, I turned right and headed north on Highway 25. But at the north edge of town, I lost my courage, suddenly feeling like I barely had the strength to even hold on to the steering wheel. Quickly turning east, I followed U.S. Highway 24 instead, driving straight into the morning sun, and leaving Colby—and the farm—far behind. For the next two-and-a-half hours, I drove more than 100 miles, zigzagging through the county roads and towns of northwestern Kansas, repeating over and over one of the main mantras from the *Land of Numb*: "Don't worry, Don. It will all work out." Finally, I pulled into Oakley, 25 miles south of Colby, and fueled up. Across the street from the gas station was the high school football field. Less than two years earlier, I had scored touchdowns on that field. I pulled up as close to the field as I could and parked the car.

I jumped out and ran to the goal line. I took a few big breaths and yelled, "Let's go, baby! You can do it!" Bending down like a sprinter, I mimicked the starter at a track meet: "Runners to your mark—pow!" I shot off across the field as fast I could run, sprinting to the far goalpost. After catching my breath, I turned, clapped my hands, and looked back at the goal line where I had started. This time I got in the 3-point stance of a football running back—legs shoulder-width apart, one hand on the grass, back straight, head up. I called signals "Three 29, Blue 87, hut-hut." Like a halfback who had found an opening in the defensive line, I ran at full speed to the goal line. As I stood there huffing and puffing, the voice of my old football coach screamed in my head, "Follis, what have been doing the last two hours driving all over tarnation? Are you going to drive out to the farm or not?"

"Yes, sir." I roared.

"Do you mean that?" he screamed.

"Yes, sir."

"I can't hear you."

"Yes, sir, Coach!"

"Then get your head in the game, boy. Act like you want it.

Now get in the car and get going—NOW! Go on! Get out of here!"

As I ran to the car, I passed an old woman standing on the track staring at me. She had heard me yelling. Ignoring her, I jumped into my car, started the engine and turned on the radio for the first time that morning. Driving straight to Colby, I exceeded the newly enacted speed limit of 75 mph. Back in Colby and on Highway 25, I kept driving north. "Come on, Follis. Move it," I said. In my rearview mirror, Colby faded from sight. Eight miles north of Colby, I turned left and followed a dirt road west for seven more. With a cloud of dust nipping at my heels, soon I saw the farm buildings off in the distance.

———

A half mile from the farm, the lump in my throat and knot in my stomach tightened, making me feel like I couldn't catch my breath. Fear gave me one more shake: "What do I do if her dad is out in the field farming and not in the farmyard? What if he is there and refuses to talk with me? What if my wife and her mother are in the house and see me pull up the lane, especially if the farmer is out in the field? Do I go up to the door and knock? Or do I spin my car around and drive back down the lane at 60 mph?"

Steeling myself, I turned onto the lane and edged the car toward the house. "Don't worry, Don," I said, repeating the morning mantra one last time. "It will all work out." A large dining room window looked out on the lane. The land is flat all around the farmstead. Anyone could have seen me coming. At the end of the lane near the house, the road veered to the right. Making a slight turn, I drove past the house without looking in the window. Finally I came to a stop next to a gray metal farm building. Beside it sat an elevated white fuel tank. To my relief, there was my wife's father, fueling his orange tractor. The rolled-up sleeves of his chambray work shirt showed his tanned, muscular arms. Without hesitating, I stepped out of the Skylark. It was 9 a.m. Waving my right hand in the air, I said in a loud voice, "Hello." When he saw me, he walked toward me, looking more surprised than I was. "Well, my goodness. What brings you out to these parts, Don?" We shook hands. Already his hand was soiled from his morning work; my hand was sweaty from all that driving.

I felt like a high school boy rehearsing for a speech class. "Good morning. What brings me out to these parts is that I drove here yesterday from Manhattan and stayed with my parents last night. I realize I came out here unannounced. I came out here hoping for a chance to talk with your daughter. Would that be possible?" She still was my wife, but I called her his daughter, somehow feeling it was the better approach if there was going to be any chance at all for me to talk with her.

"No. She does not want to talk with you," he replied. Taken aback by his curt response, I asked, "Is she here?"

"Yes, but she doesn't want to talk with you."

"How do you know?"

"That's what she told me." Pausing a few seconds, he said, "I'm sorry, but the marriage is over, Don. There is nothing for the two of you to talk about."

"Did she get my letters this month?"

"Yes. They upset her."

Back and forth we went—he with a pair of pliers hanging from a leather pouch on his belt and I in my basketball sneakers. They were shoes I purchased for basketball my senior year in high school at the end of football season but hadn't worn much. Even when I bought them, I already had decided to graduate early, forego basketball altogether, and work to make money to get married the next summer. As I pressed for more information, the farmer got done with me. Climbing back on his tractor, he removed the hose from the fuel tank and replaced the fuel cap. Pulling himself inside the cab, he started the engine.

When I stood there hesitating, he stepped back out of the cab, and said, "Don, the answer is no. You are wasting my time. You are right. I had no idea you were coming out here today. I am not going to the house to see if my daughter is willing to talk with you. I already told you the answer is no. You need to get off my land or I'll call the sheriff. I need to get out to the field. So get in your car and leave."

"Okay," I said. "I sure wish this could have been different."

"Me, too. I'm sorry it didn't work out." Adjusting his cap, he lowered himself back onto the seat of his idling tractor. He motioned with his left arm for me to drive around his tractor, then he followed my car all the way to where the lane joined the county road. After turning east onto the dirt road, I looked back at the farm, wondering what in the world had just happened. Over the past two years I had been on that farm countless times. My wife's parents were good people—hard workers, community people, committed to their Methodist church. I had eaten so many meals in their home; I helped with the farming; I had sat with them at the funeral of my wife's grandfather. As a teenage boy in love with their daughter, I was welcomed into the family with open arms, and I had walked right in. They already had raised three much older offspring. My wife had a brother who was a neurosurgeon, a brother who was an architect, and a sister who was married to a farmer and living a few miles down the road. Her parents had seemed delighted when a teenage boy with thick red hair was head over heels in love with their youngest child. But now, in less than a year, the marriage had unraveled. Turning my head from the farm back to the road, I stared into a blue sky with not a clue about what to do. Though I was proud of myself for having the guts to try again, I felt terribly confused and sad. I drove slowly back to my parents' house. As soon as I stepped inside, Mom greeted me with, "Where have you been all morning?" Her tone was sharp, way different from the night before or earlier that morning.

I replied flatly, "Just seeing some people. Just what I told you."

"I guess you aren't talking then, are you?"

"Nope. I really can't. I have a lot to think about."

"You went out to the farm, didn't you?" Evading her question, I said, "Listen, Mom. Please don't worry or ask me any more questions. I'm trying to figure things out. Things are going to be *Just Fine*. It's just going to take a while."

"I know that's where you went. Just admit it. You are going to have to get over this, Don," she said. "I just don't understand why you can't talk." Shrugging my shoulders, I walked out to the front porch, sat down on a lawn chair and breathed deeply, trying to stay calm. Instead, I sat there cursing myself: "Follis, you are a stupid idiot." Although it was pretty obvious what I was up to, I never told either Dad or Mom where I had gone. Neither of them ever brought it up again, and neither did I. That afternoon I lay on my bed, looking at Grandma's *Capper's Weekly* newspapers and staring at the ceiling. By mid-afternoon I wanted some fresh air, so I left the house and walked downtown, four blocks away. As soon as I turned onto Franklin Avenue, I literally bumped into an old high school classmate.

"So how's married life, Follis?"

"Oh, *Just Fine*."

"Holy Cow. I still can't believe you are married."

"Me neither. Well, I gotta keep going. I'll talk with you later." I turned and ran back home, shielding my face with my hands when cars passed, not wanting anyone else to recognize me.

At supper, Dad asked me if I wanted to stay and go to church the next morning before heading back to Manhattan. "Go to church?" I asked, indignantly. "No, Dad, I do not plan to stay for church tomorrow." When Dad raised his eyebrows but didn't respond, I said, "Come on Dad, think about how awkward that would make me feel. Imagine it. 'Hi there, Mr. Follis. Glad to have you at church. Where's your new wife today?'"

"Hey, I was only making the invitation," Dad said. "Obviously, do what you want." We sat there silently for a minute before Dad spoke again, this time in an authoritative tone that he rarely used. "You know something, Don, if you had listened to me in the first place, this never would have happened."

Stunned, I said, "If I had listened to you in the first place? Dad, I don't know what you are talking about." I was totally puzzled. What in the world was he saying? Not one time had he ever said anything to me about choosing to be married at age 18, as immature and ill-fated as that idea may have been. Not once! He liked my girlfriend. Her smile, lovely singing voice and teenage self-assurance attracted him. He mentioned it to me several times. Both his actions and his words toward her showed his approval.

I was completely confused and thought, "Well, I must be a terrible person to deserve a comment like that from my dad. Only a bad person would get himself into such a terrible fix." I sat there silently berating myself, calling myself awful names that were not true. Maybe Dad thought he had warned me about moving ahead too fast into a teenage marriage, but I sure don't remember it if he did. He certainly never had an 18-year-old son get married before. I'll give him that. Furthermore, Dad liked the book of Proverbs. When I was dating her, I had heard him muse over Solomon writing that no one could ever understand "the way of a man with a young woman." (Proverbs 30:19). Perhaps he knew there was no making any sense of what was happening to me. But why he would then accuse me of not listening to him, I had no idea. Who knows what emotions Dad was feeling that night? It sounded like anger. Since he always was *Just Fine*, I don't think he knew what he was feeling. He just spouted off. I'm sure he was afraid for me. He didn't know what was going to happen next, and he didn't know how to help me. Whatever happened, it would be *Just Fine*.

Years later I decided that Dad's accusation was more a matter of thoughtlessness laced with fear than it was a lack of love. Deep down he and Mom wanted life to go well for all their children, and for other people, too, including the spouses of their children. Still, so often, Dad and Mom just didn't know how to connect the emotional dots. Growing up, plenty of times I had witnessed Mom and Dad retreat to the *Land of Numb*, where they always said they were *Just Fine*. Mom was so numb when we kids asked her how she felt, she answered, "With my fingers." Talk about a conversation stopper. Now here I was not even telling them why I had come home for the weekend.

That evening, Dad and I both played our parts perfectly. I had driven home to try to do the right thing, and yet I did not have the words to even talk about it. Dad was scared; so was I. Without another word, Dad and I both got up from the table and helped Mom with the dishes. I dried and put them away while Dad swept the floor and wiped off the table, the stove, and the countertops. Moving silently around the kitchen must have zapped Dad's energy as much as it did mine—energy that might otherwise have been used to work at building a healthy father-son relationship.

Walking downstairs, I lay on Grandma's couch and watched *The Lawrence Welk Show* while she sat in her rocking chair. When I didn't say anything, she asked me, "Is something bothering you?"

"Nope. I'm *Just Fine*." Breaking into a half smile, she gave me her laugh that I had come to know all too well. It meant, "I don't believe you." The next morning when I came upstairs holding my duffel bag, Mom handed me a batch of cinnamon rolls wrapped in tin-foil she had pulled from the freezer. When we stepped outside, Dad drove the Buick into the driveway. He had fueled it, washed and vacuumed it, and wiped down the entire interior. Dad always kept the cars clean. Dad and Mom stood in the driveway next to each other as I threw my bag in the back seat and set the cinnamon rolls on the bench seat in the front. Dad said nothing about what was said around the dinner table the night before, and neither did I. With tears in her eyes, Mom hugged me, looking sad but saying nothing; Dad was stoic. He shook my hand and said, "Good luck to you."

2

ORIGINS

My junior high and high school years were spent in Colby, a town of 5,000 people, 53 miles east of the Colorado border along Interstate 70. Thirty-two miles east of Colby is Hoxie, where I was born and lived my first 10 years.

My parents, Darrel and Pat Follis, were poor farm kids raised on the High Plains of northwestern Kansas. It is where they lived their entire lives. Both are buried in the Hoxie Cemetery—Dad in 2009; Mom in 2020. Together, they rest beneath the scratchy, tough buffalo grass native to the arid High Plains. The second of five kids, I lived in a family with my older sister Darylee, younger brother Bob, sister Patti Jane and brother David—all of us born between 1953 and 1964. Mom's dad died in 1964. That's when Grandma Jennings, born in 1900, moved in with us. She stayed 17 years before moving into a nursing home the last 10 years of her life. For 45 years, Dad worked for the same public utility company, working his way up from ditch digger to district manager. His favorite Bible verse was "Work Harder." We kids told him that verse is not in the Bible.

"Well, it should be," he said. When the company said Dad had to retire, he quickly went to another company, working for another 17 years. He resigned from that job only a month before he died in May 2009 at age 81. When he died, Mom carried on, though she had lost her job—taking care of him, especially cooking him his favorite pot roast, hot rolls with butter and jam, iced tea with lots of fake sugar and homemade coconut-cream pie. After he finished eating, he'd say, "Mighty tasty." Mom fell down a flight of stairs just days before Dad died, severely injuring her brain. She was in the hospital recovering when Dad died and couldn't remember his hospital visits or his death. The injury affected her during her last decade, often leaving her confused and upset. Her whole life she, like Dad, had said she was *Just Fine*, but in her last years it was obvious she was not. In her final year she repeated the same questions. "Do you know where my home is? Do you think Dad will recognize me?" And most poignant to me, "You're a minister, Don. Do you have any idea why I'm still alive?" Next to Dad's and Mom's headstones are those of my Grandpa Charlie and Grandma Ruth Follis. Around those four headstones, I scattered some of my son's ashes, raking them into the buffalo grass with my bare hands one hot summer day. Ian died November 12, 2007, at age 21.

————

Looking back now, I wonder if some of our family secrets might have affected how Dad and Mom reacted to me about my divorce. Every family has secrets, and we had ours. I felt so much shame, I wonder about the generational shame my family carried. I saw it in both sides of the family, but it was almost never talked about. My Dad was the first-born of Charlie and Ruth Crawford Follis on January 1, 1928. Two brothers and a sister soon followed. But in fact, Dad was not Grandma Follis' first-born. That designation goes to her son Junior—J.R. as he was known. On May 25, 1925, at age 20, Ruth Crawford gave birth to J.R. Her parents raised J.R. as her brother. At the time, she lived with her brothers and parents on a farm in southwest Missouri. In a 30-page autobiography she compiled late in her life, Grandma describes hers as a "wonderful Christian family who sang and read the Bible in the evening." We knew only in whispers that something was different about J.R. and that we shouldn't ask.

Not until her 80s did my grandma tell the story about her first son's birth. She did it through letters written to Lisa, one of the adult daughters of J.R., and a cousin I barely knew. She didn't tell the rest of us. In one letter to Lisa, Grandma writes, "I'm going to tell you about your dad's father." Grandma said that he was several years older than she and from a farm family just down the road. "I didn't keep steady company with him more than 2 or 3 months. ... He never made a real commitment to me and when he found out I was pregnant, he just disappeared." That fall, Grandma wrote to Lisa, his entire family moved to Kansas City. Grandma never heard from him again. Not long after, her own parents—Isaac and Edith Crawford—left the area, too, trading their Missouri farm for one in Sheridan County in Northwestern Kansas, 450 miles away. Grandma went with them, but by early the next spring, then seven months pregnant, she traveled 400 miles back to Kansas City. On May 25, she gave birth in Vale Hospital to J.R. Crawford. On the birth certificate the line for the father's name reads *Unknown*.

After Grandma Ruth and her new baby traveled back to northwestern Kansas, her parents—then 50 years old—raised the baby as their own son and as her brother. One letter to Lisa says, "My father, loving Christian gentleman that he was, and my darling mother, did a great job of bringing J.R. up. I'm sure you will agree."

My youngest brother, David, told me he is more interested in the unknown and unspoken parts of the story. He said, "That part of Kansas was so godforsaken and sparsely populated back then, it would have been easy to keep all kinds of secrets." On my trip back in May 2022, I drove up into northern Sheridan County. My brother is right. There is nothing up there but miles of pastureland dotted with plowed fields and a very few farmsteads. As I drove along the desolate county roads, I saw only two or three people. Finally I pulled into Bow Creek Cemetery, where I walked among the grave markers of 11 Follises, including my great-grandfather Robert Follis (1864-1959).

Perhaps Grandma traveled back to western Kansas by train with the baby. We don't know, and she didn't say. But just three months after baby J.R. was born, Grandma met "a good-looking farm hand," as she described him in her autobiography. The farmhand was my Grandpa Charlie Follis. They married on February 10, 1926, when "baby brother J.R." was nine months old and living with her parents just down the road. "Charlie didn't care about seeing my folks," Grandma wrote to J.R.'s daughter. I always wondered how Grandma Follis told Grandpa Follis about her first son. Or if she did. What did she say? And then what did J.R. call my Grandma when he saw her? How did he refer to her parents who raised him? And what did he call my Grandpa Follis?

Dad told me Grandma's parents adopted J.R. He must have called them Dad and Mom. And in fact, the obituary of Isaac Crawford, Grandma's father, says he leaves "an adopted son." But my 95-year-old Uncle Norman doesn't see it that way. He told me there never were any adoption papers. "Don't go looking for them in the state offices in Topeka. You won't find any."

The memory most etched in my mind is an afternoon in 1994 when Grandma was 90. As the two of us told stories on a beautiful autumn afternoon, Grandma recalled her "days gone by," as she called them. As she regaled me with stories from her past, she still referred to J.R. as "my wonderful Christian baby brother." I almost said, "Grandma, do you want to tell me about that story?" But she was 90 years old, and I didn't press.

By then, J.R. had preceded Grandma in death; He died at just 61 in 1986. Grandma died at age 92 in 1996. Lisa told me that Grandma Follis corresponded with her dad in the last year before he died and called him several times in the hospital during the final days of his life. "I hope she said what my dad needed to hear from her," she wrote me in a letter. "... I still have some feelings of sadness and anger that my dad had to live in hiding about his real mother. ... After he died I found a lot of information he had gathered in searching for his father. So I know he always wanted to find him."

And then there's the story of my mom's birth. On November 23, 1933, my Grandpa Jennings' younger sister Lucille gave birth to her second out-of-wedlock daughter, my mom. Lucille kept her first daughter, Carole, born in 1931. My Grandpa and Grandma Jennings adopted the second baby girl and named her Patricia. Mom was their only child. Mom told me that Grandpa Jennings and Uncle Bill drove across Kansas to pick her up. When I asked Mom why Grandma Jennings didn't also go, Mom said, "I don't know. I guess there wasn't enough room for both her and me in the pickup." Mom was born in Yates Center, Kansas, where her birth mother worked as a nurse. We called her Aunt Toots. She was outgoing, drank endless cups of coffee and smoked Virginia Slims. When I was in junior high and high school, Aunt Toots came to visit several times, sleeping on the couch. She didn't visit before I was in junior high. I don't know why. When she came, my mom set out glass ashtrays. Aunt Toots was the only person who ever smoked in our house, and her cigarette butts were stained with red lipstick. If you saw Aunt Toots and Mom standing next to each other, you'd have no doubt that they were mother and daughter. Both were five-feet-eight and big-boned. Grandma Jennings was five-feet-one. But we never talked about it. A cloak of shame shrouded the visits.

When Mom was in her mid-60s, my older sister got interested in genealogy and found fascinating information about the man who probably was mom's birth father. He was a Kansas physician who traveled among the state tuberculosis hospitals, married with a family. And, of course, Aunt Toots was a nurse in some of those hospitals. But even after my sister's thorough research, Mom showed almost no interest. She finally just told my sister, "Grandma and Grandpa Jennings are my mom and dad. That's all I need to know."

And that's pretty much the way most of the information in our family came to be shared. If we asked questions, and we seldom did, the answer was always, "There is nothing else to say. We just went on with our lives." Even though Grandma Jennings lived with us for 17 years, we didn't know much about her history. We dearly loved her and she loved us. She made homemade bread, did the laundry for a family of seven, took care of the dog, and went to church with us. But we knew precious little about her background of growing up in rural North Dakota. She had six brothers, none of whom we ever met. When my brother and I asked her their names, she'd say, "Oh, I have no idea. It's not important." One day when we pushed her to come up with the name of even one brother, she snapped at us. "I don't want to talk about it." Mom called Bob and me upstairs and told us to quit asking her to name her brothers. "She had a hard life as a young girl. Please don't keep asking her the name of her brothers."

I can't help but think the things hidden and not spoken about may have mattered the most. I wish I knew more; I wish we had been better at addressing the shame and not sweeping everything under the rug; I wish there had been more closure. But at just 19, and already separated from my wife, I hadn't begun to think through what generational shame I might be carrying. That took decades. Nor did I have any idea of what skeletons might be at play in my wife's motivations in leaving me and moving on with her life. Though I never fully understood the causes and motivations of the divorce, I certainly reaped its effects. The fact was, the marriage had fallen apart in less than a year. Whatever my future now held, I had my own life to figure out. As I pulled back into Manhattan after that weekend when my wife's dad told me to get in my car and get off his land and after my own dad said that if I had listened to him, none of my troubles would have happened, I realized that the days ahead were not going to be easy for me, a young man who always was *Just Fine.*

3
DONNY DARREL

I am the curious, tenderhearted red-haired boy people called Donny Follis. Who I am today was formed out on the windy plains of Kansas. Minus the red hair, I am still Donny Darrel Follis. Even though I'm now in my late 60s, that little red-headed fellow goes with me wherever I go. He's an easy boy to be nice to, but I haven't always treated him that way. I have been plenty hard on him over the decades—often criticizing him for not being a better man. He was a lovable boy. He is a lovable man now.

In May 2022, I returned to northwestern Kansas to see my old haunts. For a week I rented an apartment in *Sheridan Acres*, a Hoxie apartment complex filled with retired folks, including my Aunt Irene Follis. My second day there a gentleman stopped me in the hallway. Forgoing any introduction, he asked, "Now what is it you are doing out here this week? Something about writing a novel about Hoxie? Your kin Irene told me something about that."

"No sir, I am not writing a novel. I am doing some research on my life, hoping to write a memoir."

"A memoir? What is that?"

"Well, it is some true stories about my life. The first 10 years of my life I lived here in Hoxie. I have come back to see what the place feels like now."

"Hmm... Well, I'll tell you something. I never have heard of anybody coming to this little town to write a memoir. So what else are you doing out here?"

Two other times I got stopped and questioned about walking up and down the streets of Hoxie. But when I mentioned my aunt's name, people responded, "Oh, so nice to meet you." Mostly, I was remembering. As I wound through the streets—passing the three places I lived those first 10 years—everywhere I looked, I saw red-headed Donny Follis riding his red Huffy bike. That kid ran that town. Taking his hands off the handlebars when he saw me, he waved with both arms straight over his head. Yep, I thought, that's my kind of boy. If only he could have stayed carefree.

On my drive to Hoxie, I crossed the Kansas state line from Colorado on a Sunday morning, immediately entering the town of the Weskan, population 158. For the next 25 minutes I drove through Weskan, Sharon Springs, Wallace, and Winona. None has even 500 people. While I fueled up in Sharon Springs, the fellow gassing his truck next to me said, "Out here the land is so flat you can see the back of your head."

Just east of Winona, I remembered a childhood event and pulled off the highway onto a narrow dirt road to record the memory in my journal. With my face buried in my notebook, I didn't notice a white pickup from the opposite direction pull alongside my car. A 70-something gentleman wearing a farm cap that read Feyh Farm Seed had rolled down his driver's window and was staring straight at me. Startled, I rolled down my window and said, "Morning, sir. How are you?"

"I'm doing fine. Didn't mean to scare you. I think the question is, 'How are you?' I thought maybe you had passed out. You doing okay?"

"Yes, sir. I sure am."

"My goodness, what in the world brings you out here to the middle of nowhere on this Sunday morning? Are you lost?"

"Nope, not lost. I grew up in these parts and I'm headed to Colby. Seeing all this vast open space triggered a childhood memory and I pulled off to write it down while it is fresh in my mind."

"Never seen anybody doing that out here. Sounds like a pretty good idea, though." His broad smile showed that one of his top front teeth was missing. "I just wanted to stop and see if you're okay. Out here in these wide-open spaces where you can see forever, believe it or not, it's easy to get turned around. You get lulled into thinking you're somewhere when you aren't, if you get my meaning. I'm just checking on you."

"Well, thank you, sir. I don't believe I'm lost. Is this your land?"

"Nope. I farm way over there." Raising his right arm from the steering wheel, he pointed with his index finger toward the western horizon. "You can't see it from here, unless you know what you're looking for."

"Thanks for checking on me. I appreciate it."

"Sure thing." Putting both hands on his steering wheel, he asked me one more time. "You sure you're going to be okay now?"

"Yes, sir. It's all good. I'll finish up a few notes and be on my way."

"You have a good day now." Nodding, he rolled up his window and headed south.

After his pickup disappeared, I slipped my journal into my backpack and pulled back onto the highway. When I came to State Highway 25, I turned left and headed north toward Colby. Suddenly my mind saw three teenagers in gray sweatsuits alongside the road. More than 50 years ago, at age 14, two of my buddies and I attempted to run a marathon on that same stretch of highway. We had convinced Mr. Beutel, our history teacher, that running a marathon—26.2 miles—was no big deal. He agreed to drive us out to our starting point on highway 25. One fall Saturday morning at 6 o'clock, we three boys, dressed in gray sweats and high-top sneakers, met Mr. Beutel in the school parking lot. He drove us along that desolate stretch of road and finally pulled over.

"Well, here we are—26.2 miles south of Colby. Good luck, gentlemen. You let me know how it goes." Turning his car around in the middle of the highway, he headed back north to Colby. One boy had brought three Moon Pies and three Cokes. I had brought a jug of water. That was it. It's hard to say who had less common sense—we boys, our history teacher, or our parents. Before starting, we found a grassy place along the ditch where we ate the Moon Pies and drank the Cokes. After we jogged about two miles, two of us got sick and ran inside an abandoned barn. When we got back on the road, a farmer spotted us walking. He pulled over and asked, "Where are you boys headed?"

"Colby," we answered in unison. "We're running a marathon."

"How is it going?"

"Not very well," I said, speaking for all three of us.

"Would you like a ride?"

After we shook our heads up and down, the farmer said, "Hop in the back." In the bed of his pickup, we sat down on loose straw mixed with cow manure. Twenty-five minutes later the farmer dropped us off in front of Colby High School.

———

When I pulled into Colby this time in a clean-smelling Honda Accord, I drove a block past the old high school before parking next to the curb at 555 West Third Street, a one-story dark brick bungalow, with a front and east porch. It's where I grew up. Peering through the open front door from my car, I saw a family eating at a table in the dining room. There was Dad sitting at one end of the table, slathering jam on one of Grandma's homemade rolls. In one of the chairs on the front porch, Tinkerbell, our dachshund, was curled up asleep, waiting for the mailman so she could growl at him for the 5,000th time. On the east side of our house, there I was with my brother Bob, playing basketball on the 8-foot goal with a broken rim and no net. And directly in front sat Dad's company car—a sparkling White 1970 Chevrolet El Camino that he took to the car wash every Saturday.

But gazing more closely, I saw only faint shadows of people inside—people I did not recognize. The basketball goal was gone. A new fence completely blocked the detached garage from sight. There were no chairs on the front porch. No dog. The mailbox that had been bolted to the bricks beside the front door was gone. After sitting silently for a few minutes, I drove three blocks to the Colby Public Library, curious as to who first settled what had become for me the *Land of Numb*. A room dedicated to showing how the town began in the late 1800s exhibited black and white pictures of settlers. Not one man, woman, or child was smiling.

"Yep," I thought, seeing the somber people, "these pioneers must be the original *Land of Numb* settlers." But wait a minute,

I thought. People with austere looks have been in pictures and statues forever. The original *Land of Numb* did not begin here. Finally, I stepped to the front desk and asked the librarian if the library had any Bibles. Walking into the stacks, she showed me 20 Bibles. Pulling one off the shelf that said *Revised Standard Version*, I sat down and read the first three chapters of Genesis.

And sure enough. There it was—the original *Land of Numb*. After Adam and Eve had eaten the forbidden fruit, God went looking for them in the cool of the evening. Having eaten the very fruit they were told not to eat—the tree of the knowledge of good and evil—Adam and Eve knew they were naked. Covering themselves with fig leaves they had sewn together, they hid among the trees.

But the Lord called to the man, asking, "Where are you?"

Adam answered, "I heard you in the garden, and I was afraid, because I was naked; so I retreated to the **Land of Numb**." And those, my friends, are the culprits, the first settlers in the *Land of Numb*. Ever since Adam and Eve stepped out of their hiding spot in the Garden of Eden and encountered God, we humans have been sewing fig leaves together, crossing our arms and telling people we are *Just Fine*. The librarian walked by and asked, "Did you find what you needed?"

"Sadly, yes."

When I told a friend about being raised in the *Land of Numb*, he said, "Hey, that's where I was raised, too. Only my home was in northern Minnesota, not northwestern Kansas." Indeed, the *Land of Numb* extends far and wide, in cities and small towns, in countries the world over. There's nothing geographical about that land.

4

STUNNED BY THE LETTER

After my long drive back to Manhattan from my unannounced trip to Colby and the farm, I never wrote my wife another letter. But in a few weeks, I received a letter from her attorney—official divorce papers. The day the packet arrived, my neighbor and I walked up to the mailbox at the same time. "What did the mailman bring you today?" he asked.

"Oh, nothing," I said, turning the letter over so he couldn't see that the fancy envelope was from a law office. The elegant black script on the cream-colored envelope read: *Mr. Don Follis,1404 Fairchild #5, Manhattan, Kansas 66502.* The return address: *Sam Lowe, General Practice Attorney, 130 W. 5th Street, Colby, Kansas, 67701.*

Though I did not know the contents, my hunch filled me with dread. Running up the three flights of stairs to my apartment, I tore open the letter. My wife was divorcing me because of "Irreconcilable Differences." Never had I even heard those words. I said them out loud—"Irreconcilable Differences." They scared me. "I'm just 19," I said out loud. "What in the world have I gotten myself into?" I thought it probably at least meant another trip back across Kansas. Carrying the letter across the street to a park, I sat down at a picnic table. For an hour, I sat nearly frozen, repeating over and over, "Boy am I in trouble now. Boy am I in trouble now." Embarrassment and shame seeped right down into my bones. I felt terrible. That evening I called my dad and told him about being served divorce papers.

"Do you think I have any options?"

With no hesitation, Dad said, "What do you mean? Of course you don't have any options. You need to come back to Thomas County and take care of business." In Dad's work at the utility company, he saw the reports of county divorces, unpaid taxes and delinquent child support payments before they were printed in the local newspaper. Now he would see news of his son's divorce. He hated to be embarrassed in front of people. He was ashamed. "You need to come back to Thomas County and take care of business."

———

As I planned my trip from Phoenix to Kansas in May 2022, I dug out the yellowed letter from the lawyer. Jennifer asked if I planned to contact my ex-wife.

Hesitating, I answered. "Oh, I doubt it. Why do you ask?"

"Why? You're writing a memoir about how you finally left the *Land of Numb*. Your first wife is central to your story. Wouldn't you want to know if she were writing a book that included you?"

"I'm sure I would."

"Well," she said, "there's your answer."

Jennifer reminded me that the whole point of going back was to get in touch with my emotions and what it felt like finally to have left the *Land of Numb*. But when I contemplated talking to my ex-wife, every part of me wanted to cross my arms and say, "Oh, I'll be *Just Fine* without doing that."

Instead, I said, "I don't even know if I could find her."

"Oh, come on, Don. I don't know anyone who can find information as quickly as you can. I bet you could find her contact information in less than 10 minutes."

I paused a few seconds more before I gave in. "Okay, I will try. You're right."

"I'm not trying to be right," Jennifer said. "But you want to write a memoir."

By the time I got to Kansas in the middle of May, I had several appointments on the calendar, including a scheduled phone conversation with my first wife. And yes, I had quickly found her email address. She agreed to set up a time to talk on the phone from her home in Oklahoma. Our conversation lasted 90 minutes. Since our 1974 divorce, we had spoken briefly one other time on the phone in 1996, when I had returned to Kansas for a funeral.

The evening we talked this time, she was just days away from celebrating her 25th wedding anniversary to her rancher husband in northern Oklahoma. They have a good marriage, she said. She talked about her Christian faith, her adult children, her grandchildren and her sister and two brothers. I spoke about marriage to Jennifer and told her about my daughter Maddie and her husband and three girls. Then I told her about my son Ian, who died when he was just 21.

It was clear that a lot of time had passed since we went our separate ways. When the conversation moved to our teenage marriage, we both realized that the decades had clouded our memories, erasing many of them and rendering the others foggy. We agreed that memory is not always reliable. As we talked, I felt compelled to ask for forgiveness for the mistakes that I had made, feeling that I had nothing to prove by trying to justify my teenage self. As I expected, I remembered some events from 50 years ago that she didn't; she recalled some that I didn't.

I remembered sitting at a little black table in a tiny third-floor apartment where I moved after she left. It's where I wrote her letters in longhand on a yellow legal pad. When I asked her about those handwritten letters, she said she had not received any such letters. There was just one from me, she said, and it was typed. She said she had returned it to me with a hand-written note across the top saying she didn't want to be contacted again.

I don't remember getting any sort of letter from her like the one she described. But I do remember something else. I didn't own a typewriter.

5
A TRIP TO THE LAW OFFICE

As I drove to Colby to sign divorce papers in late July 1974, I listened to the radio. Every station was filled with news of Watergate. President Richard Nixon's resignation was just days away. And Dad had been right. I had no choice but to deal with my business. When I pulled into Colby at 11 a.m. on a Friday morning, the house was empty except for my Grandma Jennings, who was sitting in her basement apartment, reading her *Capper's Weekly*. Before I headed to the attorney's office, I ate a sandwich and changed from my shorts and t-shirt into a pair of slacks and collared shirt. Grandma Jennings stood up, hugged me and asked, "What will happen today?"

"Grandma, I don't know exactly. I'm pretty sure I'll return in an hour a divorced man."

"That's what I was afraid of, honey."

"You don't have to be afraid, Grandma. You're about to have a redheaded 19-year-old divorced grandson. Get used to it." Seeing her blank expression, I laughed and said, "Grandma, I'm kidding."

"I love you, honey, but that's not funny."

"I've never done this before, Grandma. I guess I'll be back."

At 1 p.m., feeling anxious and numb, I walked into the attorney's office, checkbook in hand. The secretary ushered me to an office where the lawyer, Mr. Lowe, sat behind a big wooden desk. When I entered, he stood up, stepped around the desk and said, "Hello, this must be Mr. Don Follis. I am Sam Lowe. I know your Dad, but I've never had the pleasure of meeting you. I am delighted to meet you, sir. Please have a seat." He motioned to the two chairs in front of his desk. I sat in one; he sat in the other as he explained what the divorce settlement meant. When I told him the meaning of "irreconcilable differences" confused me, he said, "Don't get too hung up on the words. Those are just words we are starting to use these days. They basically mean that neither party could work out the differences in a way that would enable the marriage to go forward. Does that make sense?"

"Yes sir. I guess."

Mr. Lowe explained the divorce would be final in 60 days. "That's about it. Any questions?"

"No sir."

Mr. Lowe pulled a long black pen from its holder on his desk and handed it to me, showing me where to sign my name. With the same pen, I wrote him a check to cover my part of his fees. As soon as I handed him the check, he stood up, placed his open palm in the middle of my back and walked me to the door. Smiling, he said, "I'm glad I got to finally meet you. I like your dad. I think you wanted this, too, didn't you?"

Shrugging my shoulders, I smiled and eked out, "Thank you for your help, Mr. Lowe."

"You'll be okay, Mr. Follis."

With my copy of the divorce papers in an envelope, I stepped out of the blonde-brick office building and into the bright sunlight. At that moment, the Methodist church pastor who had officiated at our wedding walked by. He spoke first. "Well, hello Don Follis. What are you doing here in Colby on this summer afternoon?" He had seen me step out of the law office.

"Just taking care of a little business before I head back to college."

"That's good. What are you planning to do with your life?"

Hoping to quickly get out of the conversation, I said, "I'll be at the Christian college in Manhattan, trying to learn a little."

"Well, you've got to learn a little before you can learn a lot. We all have to keep learning."

"Yep, I agree."

"Good luck to you."

"And to you."

He nodded and walked on. I wondered which of us felt more awkward.

6

ALONE ON THE ROOF

When I got back to Manhattan after signing the divorce papers, I felt terrible—mostly numb about what had happened and clueless about what the future held. I am not sure I had ever even said the word grief before and I had no idea what was going on inside of me. Whatever it was, I didn't like it. I was grieving the death of my short-lived marriage. Suddenly I was a kid in uncharted territory. Not only did I not know anyone who had ever even been divorced, I did not want to talk with anyone about what had happened or what I was feeling. What was there to say? Being judged was the last thing I wanted. Fortunately, almost no one mentioned the divorce. At least to my face.

Still feeling desperate after a couple of days, I called the Methodist church in Manhattan and made an appointment to speak with the minister. During the previous year, my wife and I had occasionally attended Sunday services at the church, a stately building made of stone cut from the Flint Hills of eastern Kansas. That Tuesday afternoon, the minister welcomed this little whipped puppy to his office. After we shook hands I got right to the point. "I feel awful," I said, telling him about the divorce. "I've lost weight. Some days I don't feel like eating." After listening for a few minutes, he seemed to lose interest, which confused me. Putting some papers into his briefcase while I talked, he looked at his watch and said, "Well, I don't think I can be of much help. You seem like a very nice young man. You probably ought to see a medical doctor to make sure you are physically healthy. In any case, you need to move on with your life now. I'm sorry things fell apart for you, but now it's time for you to try to start over."

Though I had brought the divorce papers with me, I decided not to show them to him. When he stood up, I knew our appointment was over. As I started to make my exit, I changed my mind and pulled out the divorce agreement. He scanned it before saying, "I don't have anything else to say." His hand was on the door handle of his office when I said, "If I give you her phone number, would you be willing to call her? She's Methodist. Would you ask her if she would reconsider?"

"Son, you've already signed the divorce papers. I don't know her or you," he said. "There's really nothing I can do for you, except wish you all the best, and that I do. Besides seeing a medical doctor."

Had he said a counselor could maybe help me work through my grief and sadness, I might have sought some counsel, but I never did. As he walked me down the hallway to the outside door, he suggested I go to Aggieville—the campus business strip of bars, restaurants and shops next to K-State and a block from the Christian college—to meet some girls.

"Again, I am sorry. Hang in there. Your life is just getting started. You'll get another chance. It's going to get better." Shaking my hand, he turned and walked back toward his office. Driving to my apartment, I cried and swore. We Follis boys didn't cry, and it was the first time I had cried about the divorce. We were not supposed to swear either. I was zero for two that morning. But then several other sentences came out of my mouth that I had learned as a boy in the *Land of Numb*: "Pull yourself up by your bootstraps, buddy. You'll get over this in no time. Men don't cry. You're going to have to develop thick skin. Quit moping around." After a minute, I rubbed my eyes with the back of my hand and wiped my tears on my jeans. Looking at myself in the rearview mirror, I said, "Okay, Follis. That's enough. Clean up your language and get on with your day. You're going to be *Just Fine*."

That night I took the pastor's recommendation and walked three blocks from my apartment to Aggieville. Stepping inside the doorway of several bars, I looked around. The few girls I saw were sitting with guys. In one bar, two girls stood at the counter. I thought, "What am I supposed to do? Walk over to them and say, 'Hi. I'm Don. I'm 19 and divorced. This semester I will be studying for the ministry at the Christian college down the block. Would you like to have a beer?'" Feeling stupid for having taken the minister's bait, I headed back to my apartment house. The five apartments were carved from what used to be a three-story home. My third-floor bedroom window opened out to the roof. I slid a metal folding chair out onto the roof, shimmied through the window and plopped myself into the chair. With Don McLean's *American Pie* playing on my borrowed stereo, I stared into the sky until midnight. It didn't take long that summer to memorize all eight and a half minutes of that song.

> *And the three men I admire most*
> *The Father, Son and the Holy Ghost*
> *They caught the last train for the coast*
> *The day the music died*

And they were singing bye-bye Miss American Pie
  Drove my Chevy to the levee but the levee was dry
  And them good old boys were drinking whiskey and rye
  Singing, This will be the day that I die.

That one line near the end I could not get out of my mind. "The three men I admire most; the Father, Son and the Holy Ghost." I wanted to know more.

7
EIGHTEEN AND CLUELESS

I met my first wife in high school choir at the beginning of my junior year, and her senior year. She was outgoing, musically talented and confident. Within days I had a huge crush on her. She played trumpet in the pep band, while I played football and basketball and acted like I had the world by the tail. She played the guitar, and we sang duets of John Denver tunes. By the following May when she graduated, I had given her a promise ring she wore when she moved into the dorm at Kansas State that August. My senior year I graduated early, giving up basketball, which I loved. In January 1973 I enrolled with a full load of classes at the local community college and worked 40 hours a week at a Texico gas station. I lived at home, saving every dime I could for my upcoming marriage that summer. Almost every evening I worked until 11 p.m., when I closed the station. The owners told me I could take cash out of the register to buy a snack. So nearly every night I put a quarter in the pop machine and pulled a bottle of Dr Pepper out of its slot. While I ate Snickers and drank Dr Pepper I did homework, wrote love letters to my girlfriend and looked out the window, thinking about how much I was missing by not playing on the varsity basketball team with my friends.

One day a music instructor at the college who attended the Methodist church where we planned to be married stopped me in the hallway. He always had been nice to me. In a very sincere tone he said, "I know you are planning to get married here in a few months. Are you sure you kids want to get married this summer? You're awfully young. Marriage is a huge responsibility. I'm really worried for you if you jump in too soon. Just be very careful."

"Don't worry," I said, "We're being very careful. We've really thought about it." I never told anybody about that conversation, but it was the one time during the entire courtship that I doubted our plan. Because I respected the man, and he seemed to respect me, his words hit home, especially when he called us "you kids." But I put them out of my mind as I jumped into my car and drove from the community college to the Texaco station. By then the train was going one direction, and there was no stopping it. Being from the *Land of Numb*, I figured it would all work out. And so, on August 4, 1973, at the Colby Methodist church, that pretty farm girl and I married. She had turned 19 four weeks earlier; I was still 18. The sign on the back of the new car her parents gave us for a wedding present said "Just Married" as we drove off for the Colorado mountains. The sign may as well have said—*Clueless.*

Eight weeks after we were married and classes were in full bloom at K-State, I walked across the street one afternoon to Manhattan Christian College, where my older sister attended. As we sipped Cokes, she asked me what I wanted to do with my life.

"I have no idea."

"I'm sorry."

"Yeah, me too."

"I thought you wanted to be a school teacher and a coach."

"I just don't know."

While we talked, two of her classmates joined us. Both were studying for the ministry and serving little country churches, preaching every weekend. Talking to them I recalled walking to the front of the church camp chapel three years earlier and saying that I wanted to be a minister. My sister's friends suggested that I transfer colleges, telling me I could also play sports and even serve a little church on the weekends. One of them said, "I think your wife would like this place a lot, too." Walking a mile back to the one-bedroom apartment in married student housing, I thought, "That is what I want to do. My wife will like this." But that afternoon when I told her, she was baffled, completely caught off guard. It wasn't long before we recognized we needed help to communicate better and signed up for marriage counseling with a K-State counselor. In the first session my wife got right to the point, saying how confused she was about my decision to want to transfer colleges at semester and begin studying for the ministry. Turning to me, the counselor tried to figure out what it was I really wanted to do with my life. After I tried to explain myself, he said, "I'm sorry but I just don't understand why you really want to do this. Did you hear from God, or something?" He told us he never had even heard of the Christian college across the street.

"I just have a feeling," I said. "It's what I want to do. That's all I know."

"A feeling?" he asked. "We have all kinds of feelings. Is that actually hearing from God? It sounds to me like your wife does not have that same feeling." She quickly shook her head no. "Absolutely not," she said. "I do not have that feeling at all." I sat there staring at the counselor, wishing I had more words.

None came. Years later I came to understand that in the *Land of Numb* where everyone is *Just Fine*, often there are no words, especially when it comes to expressing one's deep emotions.

As we walked back to the apartment from the counseling office, I felt silly for not being able to express myself any better. Somewhere along the way I had learned just to stuff my feelings. Here I was—newly married, wanting to change horses in the middle of the stream but not able to explain my decision to anyone. I could only say, "I just have a feeling," which was embarrassing. Two weeks later her parents drove to Manhattan for the weekend. Her Dad wanted me to show him the Christian college. Sitting directly across the street from K-State, it was tiny by contrast. I felt self-conscious standing in the middle of an unpaved campus parking lot, trying to explain why I thought I wanted to be a minister. The discussion almost mimicked perfectly the one my wife and I had with the counselor. When I told him I just had a feeling that this is what I was supposed to do, he asked me, "Have you ever heard of Billy Graham?"

"Of course."

"Do you know anything about what he does?"

"Not really. He has meetings in stadiums all around the world."

"Well, yes, but how effective do you think he is?"

"I guess I don't really know."

"I think you had better do your research before you jump into this," he said. Then he raised his voice. "You completely surprised my daughter. How do you think she feels about this?"

"I don't know." At least I didn't say *Just Fine.*

"You don't know?" he asked, frustration showing. Maybe he wanted to see some fire in my belly. Maybe he wanted me to defend my decision and come right back at him, showing him I was a man who could back up what he said. Maybe he wanted me to recant and stick with the idea of being a teacher and coach. Maybe he decided he would protect his daughter. He was perplexed; I was numb. A couple of weeks later he asked my wife and me to return to the farm. We made the trip. That Saturday morning, he took me on a drive. We stopped alongside one of his fields, where for miles you could see the contour of the High Plains. He sat there telling me how he loved farming his land. "It has been a wonderful life." He asked me what I thought about learning how to farm. "Ever thought about that?"

"Not really," I said.

"I believe I can teach you, if that's something you might consider. I know my daughter would like that. Why don't you continue at K-State next semester and take some agriculture classes? Maybe you can take a class at the Christian college, too."

"I'll give it some thought," I said. His proposal scared me. When I was barely a teenager I had worked on a custom harvest crew cutting wheat and had hated it. I had worked with him while I was dating his daughter. Before we were married, I would have done anything to win his favor. But I didn't like farming. Moving back to northwest Kansas to learn to farm did not interest me.

———

One week later, I found myself cornered. I invited two students I had met from the Christian college to our apartment to talk about what it was like being a student there. At least that's what I thought I had done. My wife agreed to it. But after they arrived, one of the guys rather quickly brought up Christian baptism, which caught me off guard. The college was sponsored by the Christian Churches and Churches of Christ, a 19th century frontier church movement called the Restoration Movement. The early leaders wanted to unify the church by restoring the church based on the pattern they saw in the New Testament. Their churches emphasized their belief that baptism by immersion is essential for salvation. Some argued stridently that baptism by immersion was essential for a person to receive the Holy Spirit.

The Bible verse they point to is Acts 2:38 when the Apostle Peter gives a sermon on the day of Pentecost and 3,000 people respond, asking, "What should we do to be saved?" The Apostle Peter answered them, "Repent and be baptized every one of you in the name of Jesus Christ and you shall receive the gift of the Holy Spirit." The belief emerged that you receive the Holy Spirit after you accept Christ into your life and are entirely immersed in water. My wife had been baptized as a baby in the Methodist church and confirmed as a young girl. She felt no need to be dunked in water, feeling that she already had God's Spirit living inside her. Even though I had been baptized by immersion on Easter Sunday when I was 14, I hadn't otherwise given it much thought. Once the conversation turned into a doctrinal dispute about baptism that evening, I felt trapped. I should have nipped it in the bud and sent the two guys packing. When I let it go on, my wife felt unprotected and confused. After they finally left, I felt embarrassed by my lack of courage.

Still, when the second semester began in January 1974, I transferred to the Christian college and even joined the basketball team, just as my sister's friends had said I could. Neither my wife nor her parents wanted me there, but still I went. We stayed together in our little married student apartment but our relationship grew cold. Mostly I was so numb and confused about the future, I have little memory of the semester. The students at the Christian college knew I was married. I wore a wedding band. One night my wife came to a basketball game and sat in the stands by herself. Seeing her sitting by herself made me feel terrible. When we drove back to our apartment, we didn't talk. By the time the second semester ended, she was done with the marriage. The Friday afternoon after her last final, her parents showed up in their farm truck and loaded up her stuff. Most of what we had, they had given to us.

I knew they were coming that afternoon, so I borrowed a car from a friend and drove around town all afternoon, killing time until I headed to the burger joint where I worked on Fridays from 6 p.m. to 2 a.m. At 2:15 a.m. when I stepped back into the gray-tiled apartment and turned on the light, the place was bare, except for my clothes, a few odds and ends, and a hide-a-bed that we had purchased with my money. I stood frozen just inside the door, staring at the bare walls. Over near the refrigerator, I saw a white napkin lying on the counter. On it lay my wife's wedding ring and the opal promise ring I had given her while we were in high school. I showered and pulled out the hide-a-bed. I tied the hood of my sweatshirt over my ears. Laying on the bare mattress with no sheets or blankets, I was exhausted but wide awake. I left the lights on.

———

At 7 a.m. I was asleep when the phone rang. The lights were still on. It was my wife's dad. "Hello there, Don," he said in an upbeat voice. "How would you like to meet us all for breakfast? Then we can go to the car dealership in downtown Manhattan and take care of transferring the ownership of the car."

"I'll pass on breakfast."

"Well, okay. Meet us at the Chevrolet dealership at nine o'clock."

My heart pounded when I pulled into a parking spot at

nine. Stepping inside the show room, I could see my wife and her parents sitting in an office. Her Dad saw me and with a big sweep of his arm motioned for me to join them. When I stepped through the doorway, he smiled, stood up and shook my hand. "Nice to see you, Don." It almost felt like nothing had happened. My wife and her mom stayed seated, looking straight ahead. Nodding at them, I said nothing.

"Have a seat," a man at the desk said, pointing to an empty chair that did not match the others.

"I'll just stand," I said, self-consciously leaning against the frame of the open door. Two minutes later I signed my name on a form agreeing to turn the ownership of the car back to my wife and her dad. "Well, that's all I need," the man said, breaking the silence. Standing up, he reached across the desk and shook my hand. My wife's dad followed, standing and shaking my hand for the second time that morning. "Have a good summer," he said.

"Have a good summer yourself," I said. He patted me on the shoulder, smiled and said, "Good luck." Nodding again at my wife and her mom, I turned and left the office without saying so much as "Good-bye." I hurried to my friend's car. Driving back to the apartment, I was relieved and angry, but mostly numb. My life was changing in ways I never would have anticipated ten months earlier when I stood at the altar of the Methodist church in Colby and told a pretty girl that I was committed to her "until death do us part."

That afternoon, some guys I knew brought a pick-up to the K-State married-student housing complex and helped me move into the attic apartment the Christian college let me rent for $55 a month. As we carried the hide-a-bed up to the third floor, I remembered the words of the music instructor when he stopped me in the hallway just over a year earlier. "I'm really worried for you if you jump in too soon. Just be very careful."

PART TWO
CALLED TO THE MINISTRY

8

THE CHRISTMAS TREE

On my May 2022 trip to visit northwestern Kansas and confront any ghosts that might have hung around for 60 years, I walked up to the Hoxie Elementary School just as the bell rang, signaling the end of the school day. Students came pouring out of the building. One boy dragged his jacket on the ground as he ran. After the students had cleared, three teachers stood on the steps talking. I introduced myself, telling them I hoped that I might be able to go up to the second floor and look inside my old fourth-grade classroom, if in fact it still existed. Pointing to the second floor, I said, "It was right across the hall at the top of the stairs. But that was 60 years ago."

"You'll never believe it. That's my classroom," one of the teachers said. "And it's a fourth-grade classroom."

"Incredible." I smiled, shaking my head.

"You're supposed to check in at the office, but the students are all gone. Go on up. I'm headed down to the office. I'll tell them. What is your name?"

"Don Follis," I said. "I appreciate your help."

"Oh, I know the Follises here in Hoxie. Are you related?"

"I am."

"How long has it been since you were in this building?"

"Sixty years."

"Sixty years? Oh, my goodness. Go on up and take a look around. I'll write your name down in the visitor book in the office."

I climbed 18 stairs. Sure enough, the old classroom had not gone anywhere. Just as I remembered, it was across the hallway from the top of the stairs. Standing in the middle of the doorway, I counted 20 desks. On the back row, near the coat closet, sat 3 desks all by themselves. I knew the little redheaded boy with a burr haircut who sat in the middle desk in the back row in 1964—me.

While I watched a janitor empty the trash, the deep voice of Miss Dorothy Karnes seeped into my memory. She was my fourth-grade teacher. The May 2022 calendar on the wall changed to December 1964. On Friday, December 4, 1964, Miss Karnes asked me to skip recess after lunch and ride in her car to go pick out the class Christmas tree. But believe me, it was not because I was the teacher's pet.

Just before lunch that day, Miss Karnes had each student read out loud from the fourth-grade reader. Working her way from front to the back, Miss Karnes stood beside each desk while the student read. When she reached the last row, where three boys waited to read, Miss Karnes asked David, the boy on my right, to proceed. David could barely read. He butchered nearly every word while Miss Karnes painstakingly pulled him along. As teacher and student struggled, the boy to my left and I giggled. Suddenly the dam broke and we burst into full laughter. Whether I was or not, Miss Karnes decided I was the culprit.

"David, stop reading," Miss Karnes said loudly. Moving 36

inches to her right, she stood directly in front of my desk. She seemed six feet tall.

"Mr. Follis, please look at me." As she peered down at me, I buried my face in my book, completely frozen. The room fell silent. "Donny Follis, please look at me when I speak to you." When I raised my head, the giant woman said, "Do not *ever, ever, ever* (accentuating *ever* with greater emphasis each time) make fun of someone who is trying his best to read. You know better than that, don't you?"

I did not move as Miss Karnes slowly backed away, turned and walked to the front of the classroom. Neither of us gigglers got a chance to read. "Close your books," she said to the class disgustedly. "We are going to lunch." Looking to the back row, she threw out one final barb. "Next time, I hope you two boys will know better." After lunch, we zipped up our coats, pulled on our gloves and headed outside to play. Unexpectedly, Miss Karnes came up behind me. When I glimpsed her, I froze, but this time she was all smiles—as gentle as one of Santa's elves. With a twinkle in her eye she whispered, "Come here a second. I need a little help, Donny. What do you say instead of you going out to recess, you and I go over to Getz's IGA and pick out a Christmas tree for our classroom? We can go right now. Sound fun?"

Sound fun? Just the two of us? Six-foot Goliath and nine-year-old me whom she had crushed only 25 minutes earlier? Fun? It sounded like torture. And yet, the next thing I knew I was in Miss Karnes' car riding to the grocery store. She parked directly in front of an entire wall of pine trees leaning upright against the cinder-block building. When we stepped out of her car, she pointed to the trees. "Look at those beauties. Which one do you think we should get? Pick the one you like, Donny."

Grabbing the first tree my nine-year-old hand touched, I held it up.

"Is that the one you like?"

"Yes, ma'am."

"Hold onto it while I go inside and pay." Grasping the tree, I moved it in front of me, trying to hide my face, hoping no one would see me. "We got a good one, Donny," Miss Karnes said, after we put it in her trunk and drove back to the school. As we carried it up the 18 stairs, the students from our class were returning from noon recess. Without warning, David was to my left.

"Where have you been?" he asked.

"Nowhere," I said.

"You went and got a Christmas tree didn't you?" It was obvious. Feeling embarrassed, I thought that David should have been asked to help pick out the tree. But I was the one holding the tip of the tree, while Miss Karnes held the trunk. Standing in the doorway of the classroom nearly 60 years later, I mused about the incident. Miss Karnes surely felt guilty for coming on so strong. Her sympathy had not made me feel any better. But what was I supposed to say when she asked me to go with her to pick out the class tree?

After seeing the old classroom that afternoon, I looked up Miss Karnes' teaching career. I found a group picture that included many of my elementary school teachers. In it, Miss Karnes was not six feet tall. She was stout and about five-feet-six-inches. But in my memory, she is larger than life. Her words melted little Donny Follis right onto the floor. When she exploded, I retreated to my safe place, the *Land of Numb*. At age nine I never even had heard of that land, of course, but my little self already knew how to go there.

9
A PROPER GOOD-BYE

A month after I got to pick out the class Christmas tree, Miss Karnes organized a going away party for me on a cold January Friday. Dad's job was moving us 30 miles away to Oakley, a town I had never heard of and never visited. It was twice as big as Hoxie.

After class, Miss Karnes handed me a brown paper bag and told me to clean out my desk. "Set the textbooks on my desk. Put everything else in the sack and take it home." She needed to walk down to the school office, which left me alone in the classroom with Kim, my long-time friend. Standing to my side straight as a pencil, Kim did not say a word. Out of the blue, I turned to him and told him to go get Debbie Fromme, a girl in my class I liked. Her dad was an attorney, and Debbie was pretty, smart, and poised.

"I want to kiss Debbie Fromme good-bye, Kim. Go get her." Without hesitating or saying a word, he bolted out of the classroom and ran down the hallway like a faithful scout. In an instant, he was back with Debbie Fromme at his side. There she stood in the classroom doorway bundled up in her red coat and red hat, looking directly at me.

"Oh, I didn't mean it," I said.

"What?" she asked in a puzzled voice.

Speaking louder, I said, "I didn't mean it."

With that, she left as quickly as she had appeared. Walking back to my side, Kim said, "I told her you just wanted to talk with her." Never had I kissed any girl, and I didn't want to kiss Debbie Fromme. My scout got it right. I wanted to talk with her and say a special good-bye—to her alone. I wanted her to remember me. Standing in that classroom 60 years later, I had the words I did not have that January day in 1965. When the janitor moved to the next classroom, I walked to the front of the room, nervously cleared my throat, looked at the doorway where she stood 60 years ago and said:

"Debbie Fromme, I want to say a special thank you to you for being my friend. That's why I asked Kim to go get you. You are smart and nice and a leader, and I admire those qualities. I saw you help the other students with their projects. You are kind and patient. Thank you for being such a good influence on our class, and on me. You are a good person. Good luck in the future. Good-bye for now! I know you are going to make the world better for all of us."

The teachers were still talking when I stepped outside. "How was it?" asked the fourth-grade teacher.

"Thanks for asking. It went pretty well," I said. "The old room and I had a few words. All good, though, because I got to have my say." I smiled as I walked to my car, knowing that when Donny Follis called Debbie Fromme back to the classroom to kiss her, he was on a journey, unbeknownst to him, to one day leave the *Land of Numb* and to become more fully human.

10

DO YOU BOYS BELIEVE?

In early February 1969, our eighth-grade basketball team won the Northwestern Kansas league championship. In a picture that made the front page of the Colby Free Press, I am kneeling with one hand holding one side of the trophy. My friend Jeff Knudson is grasping the other side. We were a force to be reckoned with, albeit an inconsistent one. Nearing the end of the season after one of our opponents scored, I threw the ball in to one of my friends, who took one dribble before promptly scoring a lay-up ... for the opponent.

The week after the championship game, a city-wide Christian revival meeting began at the community building in downtown Colby. The five-day event featured Bill Glass, a professional football player who also was an evangelist. On our calendar in the kitchen, Mom put a big X through every day of the week. We attended every night. The first night, the crusade team taught a song whose words and tune still are etched in my mind. "Jesus Christ is the way. Jesus Christ is the truth. Jesus Christ is the life and he's mine, mine, mine."

Thursday morning, Mom said to me, "You realize that

tonight and tomorrow are the last two nights?" I knew she wanted me to walk to the front when Evangelist Bill Glass gave the invitation to accept "Jesus Christ as your personal Lord and Savior." Sure enough, that night when he called for public decisions, my friend Steve Bugbee and I walked to the front. He stepped out first; I tucked myself in right behind him. About 20 others made their way to the front. It was not unlike what I had seen at the Billy Graham Crusades on television, watching along with my Grandma Jennings down in the basement.

Standing near the stage, a gentleman approached Steve and me, shook our hands and asked, "Are you boys here to accept Jesus Christ as your Lord and Savior?"

"We are." Taking a notecard from his front pocket, he read: "I have only two questions for you. Do you boys believe that Jesus Christ is the Son of God?"

"Yes, we do."

"Do you turn from your lives of sin and accept Christ by faith into your hearts?"

"Yes, we do."

The man slid the notecard back into his shirt pocket protector behind the pens. He shook our hands and said, "Welcome to the family of God, boys." As we drove home, Dad and Mom only said, "Congratulations." Though I had been raised in the church, and certainly considered myself a Christian, that night was the first time I had made a public profession of my faith.

For the next six weeks, a star high school athlete named Scott Andrews visited me at our home to follow up from the crusade. He wore his Colby High School black and orange letter jacket with an eagle emblazoned on the front. Mom had us sit at the kitchen table and made sure no one interrupted us while we met. He sat beside me each week as together we filled out answers in a workbook that explained the basics of the faith.

Some nights Scott sketched out his favorite basketball plays in the back of my workbook. One night we talked about track season. Scott drew an oval track in my booklet and explained his strategy for how he ran the two-mile race in 10 minutes, 20 seconds, during the league meet of his junior year. On Easter Sunday I was baptized by immersion at our church along with my 12-year-old brother Bob and two other boys the same age as us.

———

Just days after my baptism, I visited one of the boys who had been baptized along with me. We rode our bikes to the edge of town where he proudly showed me some enormous farm machinery—two gray Allis-Chalmers combines with black trim sitting beside two grain trucks. They towered over my head. His dad was a custom grain harvester. The wheat in the United States ripens from south to north—in Oklahoma in early June and in the Dakotas in late July.

My friend asked me if I wanted to be part of a grand adventure, joining their harvest crew that summer. He said he'd drive the pickup and pull the camper while I sat in the cab with him. After listening to his son and me make our appeal, the harvester agreed to have me on the crew. He was a church deacon and assured my Dad and Mom that his 14-year-old boy and I would work together. Furthermore, the three of us would all sleep in a camper each night. Dad and Mom hesitated but gave their blessing. Before the crew left in early June, I obtained a permit that allowed 14-year-old Kansas teenagers to operate farm equipment.

For nine weeks, along with a crew of seven others, mostly college boys, I learned to operate a combine and drove it through wheat fields from Oklahoma to South Dakota. At night the crew sat around a fire and drank beer. Coming from a home where there was no alcohol, that surprised me. To get me settled, Dad took vacation our first week out, joining the crew. One night Dad stood next to the boss on the other side of the fire from where I sat on an overturned plastic five-gallon bucket. While I watched the fire and listened to the crew members tell stories, the boss handed Dad a can of Hamm's beer. Never had I seen dad drink. He opened the can but just held it, taking only a sip or two. When I went over and stood beside him, he whispered, "This stuff is just awful."

Since I had just completed my booklet on how to begin the Christian life, I brought it along with my King James Version Bible. Scott Andrews, my mentor, called the Bible his sword. "Always keep your sword with you," he said. Early one morning a college boy on the crew saw me sitting on the overturned bucket with my booklet and my Bible in my lap. "I don't think you're going to need those this summer, pal," he said, smiling. Immediately I went inside the camper and stuffed them in the bottom of my duffel bag, where they remained the rest of the summer.

———

By late July I was homesick and tired of driving a combine through "the amber waves of grain," however grand the song *America the Beautiful* makes them sound. The job was not nearly as romantic as the song. I missed swimming in the city pool, playing baseball, and teasing girls in the park. In late July, as the job drew to a close, we made our way north, crossing the Nebraska/South Dakota border and pushing into the Rosebud Indian Reservation. The harvest crew traveled in a caravan. The boss led the way with a combine chained atop the bed of the truck he drove. Others on the crew followed.

The boss's 14-year-old son brought up the rear, driving the pick-up and trailer we slept in. I rode with him. Suddenly, the rig in front of us veered to the right, dipping down into a deep ditch along the highway. We two 14-year-olds watched the rig go airborne and nosedive into a pasture, creating an enormous cloud of dust. When the front of the truck slammed into the pasture, the chains securing the combine to the truck bed snapped, sending the combine tumbling over the truck cab, flattening it and trapping the driver to the floorboard. We jumped out of the pickup and ran toward the smashed truck, yelling the name of the college kid trapped on the floorboard.

The boss was in the lead truck. When he realized what had happened, he pulled over his rig and ran a half mile back to the site of the accident. By then, several cars had stopped and a half dozen people surrounded the crushed truck. We could hear the driver moaning. A family headed to the Black Hills pulled over in their camper. The wife was a nurse and she started telling us what to do. As soon as we got the injured crew member out of the truck and into the back of the family camper, the dad driving the camper turned it around and headed 25 miles back to Valentine, Nebraska. The injured college boy was covered with dust and blood, going in and out of consciousness. The nurse tended to him in the back of the camper. The young man broke his pelvis and had cuts and bruises all over his body, but he lived. The truck and combine were destroyed. Cans of beer stored on the truck were strewn across the pasture. We two 14-year-olds scoured the pasture, picking up every can of beer we saw and throwing them in the back of the pickup before our entire crew turned around and headed back to Valentine. Late that evening, the boss sent his son and me to take the beer we had retrieved, drive down along the Niobrara River that skirted the north edge of Valentine, and "throw it somewhere in the weeds. Just get it out of here."

The next day we headed back to Kansas to regroup and get more equipment. While I was home for a couple of days I told my Dad I didn't want to go back. He didn't hesitate. "You'll be okay. You made a commitment. You've got to finish now." A few days later we were back at it, heading north to South Dakota with a different truck and a new combine. The injured crew member's mother drove to Valentine, retrieved him, and took him back to Kansas. The boss hired a new driver. When we reached Valentine, the boss pulled his rig into a truck stop while the other drivers pulled in behind him. He came over to the pickup and told his son to scoot to the middle, while he drove us down to the Niobrara River to the place where we had thrown the cans of beer. When we pointed to the spot, he told us to retrieve as much beer as we could find in the tall grass. "A guy needs a beer every now and then. Put it in the cooler," he said. After we got back into Valentine and packed the beer in ice, he said, "Let's keep rolling."

We arrived at the wheat farm of our final customer late in the afternoon on July 21, 1969. The farmer invited the entire crew into his house that evening to watch Neil Armstrong walk on the moon. Along with his family, we huddled around a black and white television, watching Armstrong step out of the Apollo 11 lunar module and onto the moon's surface. On July 28 we finished cutting the last wheat field and on Saturday, July 30, the boss dropped me off at my home. "Send me your hours so I can settle up with you," he said. I had no idea what that meant. It was the first time he ever mentioned keeping track of how much I had worked. When the boss saw my blank look, he said firmly, "Just do the best you can and let me know. Otherwise, how will I know how to pay you?" I still didn't get it. Hadn't I been with him every day? Hadn't he seen me struggle with the tools and equipment I knew nothing about? He was exasperated. "Just do the best you can," he said. "Look at a calendar. We left June 4; today is July 30. It's not that hard." When I still didn't say a word, he sighed and said, "You know, Don, you're the first kid who has ever worked for me I couldn't teach how to do this job."

While he drove off, I carried my duffel bag up the sidewalk to our brick bungalow. Grandma Jennings was sitting on the porch in her favorite lawn chair. Tinker, our dachshund, was asleep under her chair.

"Hi Grandma," I said, as Tinker woke up and sniffed my ankles.

"Well, my stars," she answered. "What brings you here?"

"I'm back."

"You don't look very happy about it."

"I'm *Just Fine*." I didn't tell her what had just happened. But as soon as I stepped into the house and greeted Dad and Mom, I immediately told them about totaling up my work hours and sending them to the boss. "He said to add up my hours for the whole summer by looking at a calendar. He said it should be easy to do. What should I do?"

"Don't do anything," Dad said.

"Would you call him and see what he meant?"

"No. We don't need to ask him anything. He'll make it right. Don't worry about it. You're just going to have to be patient. He's been through a lot in the last month, especially trying to sort through things after that wreck. You'll get paid." I mentioned nothing about the boss saying that I was the first kid who ever worked for him that he couldn't teach to do the job. With his response, Dad's *Land of Numb* philosophy was in full view—if at all possible, don't make waves. All conflict is bad. This is just one of those things. On that philosophy, Dad and Mom totally agreed. The underlying reason was clear. If you courageously speak the truth, people might not like you. Why would anyone jeopardize being liked?

Dad didn't ever call the boss, and I'm positive he never mentioned anything about it when he saw him in church. I finally did get paid, but the money didn't come for nearly two months, well into October. Freshman football season was nearly over when a check came in the mail for $339.16. Even though I had nearly forgotten about it, when I opened the envelope and saw the check, I said, "This amount is too low."

"You don't know that," Dad said when he got home from work. When I told Mom that I should write the boss a note saying I had worked for a thousand hours and the check was several hundred dollars short, she said, "Very funny."

———

Though I saw my first boss at church after that first summer job, we rarely talked. When our paths did cross, we both just nodded. Occasionally he spoke, saying, "How you doing, pal?" I replied with the answer I had heard my whole life, "*Just Fine*, thank you." Eight years later when I graduated from college with a ministry degree, the church elders asked me to speak at a Sunday evening service. To my surprise, the old boss was there that night. As I stood at the door to greet people following the service, he was the first to step toward me. Sticking out his right hand he smiled and said, "Congratulations. I never thought you could do it."

"Well, I guess I did," I said. He merely nodded and smiled as he walked out the door. I never saw him again. Life went on with the conflict unresolved in my mind until one afternoon 12 years into my Illinois campus ministry. That October Sunday after I had spoken at a church an hour east of Urbana, I meandered home along the back roads. Lots of farmers were harvesting corn and soybeans. I thought of the old boss. Suddenly, I began smiling, realizing that somewhere along the way I had forgiven the man.

"Well, old boy," I said out loud as I watched the combines mow down the corn, "The Lord bless you and keep you; the Lord make his face shine on you and be gracious to you whatever you are doing these days; the Lord turn his face toward you and give you peace." Rolling down my window, I let the warm October breeze hit my face. My first boss needed my love way more than he needed my hate. Somewhere along the way I had stepped off the escalator of revenge.

11
I WANT TO BE A PASTOR

We Follises always work. The summer after driving through the wheat fields in Oklahoma, Kansas, Nebraska and South Dakota, I bused tables at the Ramada Inn restaurant, where the spilled macaroni salad made its way into the shag carpet. Mid-summer, the restaurant manager gave me a break so I could I attend church camp 100 miles away. I was about to make a decision that would affect the rest of my life.

At camp I met several Bible college teams that were there recruiting potential students. One girl named Paula had just finished her freshman year at a Bible college in Nebraska, and she made it clear to me that I should be a pastor. She loved to read the Bible and spent the week trying to make me a Bible reader. I was smitten with Paula, who was four years older than I, so I was more than willing to read the Bible with her. One afternoon while the other campers played softball or swam in the lake, Paula asked me if I wanted to sit under a picnic shelter and read the Psalms together. She said the right words when she smiled and proclaimed, "I think you would make an outstanding preacher. You are easy to talk to and a good conversationalist." When one of the campers ran by and told me to get my ball glove and get on the field, I told him I was going to read the Psalms with Paula.

"Really?" he said. "That's weird."

Each meal I lined up next to Paula and sat beside her. Near the end of the week, she finally said, "I like you, Don, but you need to find some other people to sit with this time."

The final night featured a talent show, followed by a Vespers service in which campers were challenged to consider God's call on their life—responding to whether they believed God was calling them into the ministry as their life vocation. My older sister, Darylee, was also at the camp, and that afternoon she convinced me to sing a solo during the talent show. In the late 1960s as the Jesus Movement spread across the country, lots of Christian tunes became popular, including the one I sang that night: *God Fills the World*. Darylee is a good pianist and had brought the sheet music. Though we practiced that afternoon in the camp chapel after I finished reading the Psalms with Paula, when the talent show was about to begin, I said to my sister, "I'm pulling out. I can't do it."

"You'll do great," she insisted.

"I changed my mind. I can't do it."

"I'm your older sister. You are doing it. Please. It will be good. Please."

"Well, okay, but I am not going to stand on the stage. I'm going to stand right beside the piano." Translation: I am going to hide behind the piano. When it was our turn, I followed Darylee up the aisle to the piano, my feet scuffing along the concrete floor. Darylee sat down at the bench and I stood beside her. The campers, largely kids from small-town churches in northwestern Kansas, had dressed up for the final night. I could smell Brut cologne. The doors at the back were wide open, allowing a breeze to flow through the chapel on that warm night. I wanted to walk out of the chapel onto the prairie and disappear. Instead, I nodded to my sister and she began playing. *God Fills the World* had a tricky beat, but we had worked it out when we practiced that afternoon. My entry was good, but before long I got ahead of her and we both knew it. I quit singing. Darylee quit playing.

With 100 sets of eyes looking at us, I said, "I messed up. Sorry." Bending down to my sister's ear, we conferred, whispering. No one moved. Pointing to the sheet music sitting on the old upright piano, Darylee put her finger on the spot where the chorus began and said, "Why don't you just try the chorus again, and we'll end with that." And that's what I did. The campers roared their approval, surely feeling more relief for me than appreciation for the music. When we sat down, my sister bent over and whispered, "It's okay." My embarrassment was short lived because the next thing I knew, the talent show was over and the Vespers service was in full swing. After an impassioned sermon, the preacher asked those who felt called to make the ministry our life's vocation to come toward the front. The tune *God Fills the World* had given way to *I Have Decided to Follow Jesus* as my sister and I joined 15 other high school campers who had gone forward. After three rounds of the chorus, the camp dean raised his hand, stopping the pianist and the singing. Scanning the room he said, "If you don't believe those words—'I have decided to follow Jesus'—don't sing them. If you do mean them, then sing them with all your heart. If in your heart God is calling you to make a decision tonight, there should be nothing stopping you. Tonight, God is calling some of you to make a decision that will reverberate throughout all eternity."

I might have messed up my cue earlier trying to sing *God Fills the World*, but I did not want to miss making a decision that could reverberate throughout all of eternity. So I went forward. Some were crying; I was stoic. After I got up to the front, I wasn't sure why I was there. The music stopped, and the camp dean asked each of us at the front to declare why we had come forward. Most proclaimed that they wanted to be ministers or missionaries. A few rededicated their lives to the Lord. Two boys spoke before me, both merely saying, "I want to be a minister." I repeated exactly what they said. My older sister announced that she wanted to be a missionary.

"There is no such thing as full-time Christian service," the camp dean said. "We all are called to serve the Lord full time. But the Lord gives some a specific call to make the ministry their life's vocation. This is what these fine folks at the front have done tonight. Are there more? Surely the answer is yes." I didn't even know what the word vocation meant. As we sang *I have Decided to Follow Jesus* one more time, one other camper stepped out and came to the front.

After all the campers at the front had explained their decisions and the service ended, my church pastor—serving on the camp staff that week—caught up with me as I walked in the dark toward the boys dorm. I didn't see him until he put his hand on my shoulder and said, "Don, my goodness. Congratulations. You have decided to become a minister. Good for you."

"Thanks."

"Don't worry about the talent show. You have made a great decision to become a preacher. Your Dad and Mom will be proud." With his arm around my shoulder, he told me about the time he decided to become a preacher in rural Oklahoma in the 1950s. He said when he told his Dad—who was not a Christian at the time—his Dad responded, "You'll be a helluva minister." I thought that was a crude way of saying it, but at least I thought it was positive.

Interestingly, though, years after my boyhood minister had

died, his son told me a different version of that story. "My Dad really liked you. And yes, that is what he told you his own Father said, but there is more to that story you don't know." The son said the night his dad made a decision to become a minister, he knocked on his father's bedroom door to announce his decision. But his father actually responded derisively, saying, "A helluva minister you'll be." The son then said to me, "The night you made your decision, Dad changed the order and tone to make it positive."

Following up his optimism, my pastor paused outside the boys dorm and asked me, "Why don't you preach next Sunday evening? I think that would be great."

"Sure," I said, "I'd love it." And that's how it all started for the boy who had never spoken in front of people and had never read the Bible other than a few assorted verses here and there, including those Psalms with Paula earlier that week at church camp. Who knew that at age 15, if you stood in front of 100 or so teenagers in northwestern Kansas, declaring that you felt called to one day be a pastor, then by gum, you might find yourself the very next week in the pulpit declaring the word of the Lord. If only it had worked that way later on in my life. Though I was welcomed as a novice preacher at age 15, as a divorced 19-year-old who was determined to study for the ministry, I discovered it was not always that way.

12

THE PREACHER IS IN THE HOUSE

Days after church camp, I was back busing tables at the Ramada Inn. One of the waitresses with red hair like mine was having a smoke out behind the kitchen when I walked by. Earlier that summer she offered me a cigarette and I tried it while she and another waitress smoked. When I coughed my head off, she laughed and said, "Once you smoke a few more, your lungs will get used to it." I decided my lungs did not need to get used to that. I never smoked again.

"You're back from church camp," the red-headed waitress said. "How was it? Pretty fun?"

"Yeah," I said.

"What part did you like the best?"

"I decided to become a minister."

"A minister? Wow. I've never known a preacher. From a busboy to a preacher. What do you know?"

"I'm actually going to preach this Sunday evening."

"Wow," she said a second time, "What will your sermon be about?"

"Oh, I don't know. Probably something from the Bible."

"What's your favorite part of the Bible?"

"Oh, I don't know. I mostly like all of it."

"Well move over Billy Graham," she said, flicking her cigarette onto the ground.

That next Saturday morning I bought new football cleats for the coming season and was about to go outside to play basketball on our driveway when Mom popped her head out the door and said, "Don, aren't you scheduled to give a sermon tomorrow night at church?"

"Oh yeah, Mom. I need help." I hadn't forgotten but was doing all I could to avoid it.

"You had better get in here, right now." Throwing the basketball into the back yard, I walked downstairs and plopped down at Grandma Jennings' yellow Formica kitchen table. "Mom," I yelled upstairs to the main kitchen. "I'm ready for your help."

Dad was an elder in the church, but Mom was the go-to person for emergencies. I did not have a clue about how to write a sermon and my stomach was churning. Mom came downstairs holding her Revised Standard Version Bible. She set it on the table alongside my black King James Bible, the one I could zip open and shut. A silver cross dangled from the zipper tab. Beside the two Bibles I placed a book of quotations from famous people, which I had pulled from our bookshelf. Grandma handed me a pen and two sheets of lined notebook paper.

"How can I help?" Mom said, stepping into the kitchen.

"Mom, sit down."

"Just calm down. How about, please sit down."

"Mom, please just sit here." After sitting quietly for a few seconds, Mom said, "Well, I am here."

"Thank you. I need some help."

"What do you want to say tomorrow in your sermon?"

"What am I supposed to say?"

"Well, honey, you are the one speaking. Whatever the Lord has put on your heart."

"I don't have anything on my heart, Mom."

"Why don't you just tell about making the decision to become a minister while you were at camp last week and read a few Bible verses. Take two or three minutes. That will be plenty."

"No, Mom. This is supposed to be a sermon."

"Telling people about your decision would be a good sermon. We are on a short deadline, young preacher who totally forgot about it."

"Mom, please help me."

"Shall we call the pastor and ask what he expects?"

"Mom, he expects a sermon. That's what he said. I don't want to call him."

With me on one side of the yellow table, and Mom on the other, we brainstormed. She turned to Psalm 23 and told me to read it. After reading it silently, I looked up. "I like it," I said.

"Me too. Let's start with that."

On the top line of my notebook paper I wrote: "Read Psalm 23."

"How about something from the first chapter of the book of Genesis?" she asked.

"Sounds great," I said. Mom turned to Genesis chapter one and handed me her Bible. I read, "In the beginning God created the heaven and the earth."

"That's a good verse, Mom."

"Yes, it's always good to start at the beginning." Mom was doing her best to affirm me. After I wrote down the Genesis reference, Mom handed me her Bible and said, "Turn to I Corinthians 13. That's the love chapter." When I couldn't find it, Mom said, "Look in the table of contents." When I found it, we decided reading verses four through seven was plenty. "Stand up and read it right now. I want to hear your speaking voice."

"Mom, I don't want to do that here in Grandma's kitchen."

"If you're going to preach, you have to be able to read the Bible well. There are good acoustics in here." Standing in front of Grandma's rounded-corner Frigidaire refrigerator, I held Mom's Bible in both hands, cleared my throat, and read:

> *4 Love is patient and kind; love is not jealous or boastful; 5 it is not arrogant or rude. Love does not insist on its own way; it is not irritable or resentful; 6 it does not rejoice at wrong, but rejoices in the right. 7 Love bears all things, believes all things, hopes all things, endures all things.*

"Read it again," she said. "Big voice. Let's go."

"Once was enough."

"Read-it-again, son!" When I finished, she said, "Your voice was stronger the second time." Picking up the book of famous quotations, I showed Mom quotations from Winston Churchill and Abraham Lincoln. "You don't really need quotations from famous people in your sermon."

"But I like these," I said.

"Well, okay," she said, shaking her head. "Write them down." For the next few minutes I copied these Churchill words out of our book of famous quotations:

> *This is the lesson: never give in, never give in, never, never, never, never—in nothing, great or small, large or petty—never give in except to convictions of honour and good sense.*

Mom rolled her eyes. Her patience was running thin. "If you tell them about why you made your decision to be a

minister and read the verses and these two quotations, that
will be a big plenty."

"Mom, I think we should end with a verse from the book of
Revelation." Sighing, she turned to Revelation 21 and pointed
to verses six and seven, which she again had me stand and read
in front of the refrigerator:

> [6] *And he said to me, "It is done! I am the Alpha and the Omega,
> the beginning and the end. To the thirsty I will give from the
> fountain of the water of life without payment.* [7] *He who conquers
> shall have this heritage, and I will be his God and he shall be
> my son.*

"Good job," Mom said, "I think you have it. Go over your
notes a couple of times. Put a little piece of paper in your Bible
marking each verse. You don't want to get lost trying to find
the verse you want to read. You'll be fine." Standing up, but
leaving her Bible on Grandma's table, she walked back
upstairs.

"Wait Mom," I said. "Will you iron my white shirt?"

"No," she snapped. "You are not wearing a shirt and tie,
son. You are a layman. You are 15 years old. No one expects you
to dress up."

———

My minister introduced me the next evening, explaining that I
had made a commitment at camp to one day be a preacher.
"This is his first sermon. Please give him your full attention."
Bending over to Mom, I whispered, "See what I told you. It's a
sermon." I had brought a stop watch from home, which I
handed to Mom. "What are you doing with that?" she asked.

"I just want to know how long I preach." Mom pursed her

lips, but when I walked to the front and stood behind the pulpit, she held the stopwatch chest high, like a track official at the finish line at a track meet.

"Good evening, everyone," I said, "I'd like to read from the Bible." After that stirring introduction, I read Psalm 23, quickly moved to the verses in Genesis chapter one, then on to the verses on love in I Corinthians chapter 13. The quotations from Winston Churchill and Abraham Lincoln were next. The Churchill quotation was the famous one about never giving in. The Lincoln quote was "I am not bound to win, but I am bound to be true." How those quotations fit after the love chapter, I have no idea. I just liked the words. The sermon ended as I read from Revelation chapter 21. Everyone clapped as I walked off the stage. After I sat down— utterly relieved—I bent over and asked Mom, "How long did I preach?"

"Five minutes, 40 seconds."

"Five minutes, 40 seconds? That can't be right."

"Okay, then, I'll give you six minutes." Six minutes it was. My pastor came back up to the pulpit and said that because several teenagers who had gone to camp were present that evening, he wanted to give them a minute to share a highlight from their week. After two or three kids spoke, a girl named Michelle stood and looked around at the 50 faithful.

Grasping the pew in front of her with both hands, she had a stern look as she said, "Camp made me realize that I am not taking my faith seriously. I rededicated my life to the Lord, and things are going to change." After hearing a couple of "Amens," she continued. "The faith of some people here tonight is a lot like a soggy Kleenex. This place needs to change." Immediately, the pastor jumped up and said, "Thank you, Michelle. We surely all need to be open to making changes in our lives." As Michelle sat down, she added, "I really mean it." The pastor thanked everyone for sharing and brought the service to an end with a benediction.

After church, Dad said nothing about my six-minute sermon but talked about how disgusted he was when Michelle said that the faith of the adults in the church was a lot like a soggy Kleenex. "It is fine that you kids make commitments to serve the Lord, but you don't say something like that. That's ridiculous." On the 20-minute drive home, I rolled my sermon notes into a tube and slapped it against my leg, pretending I was a drummer. Sitting beside me in the third seat of our white 1963 Ford station wagon with red vinyl interior, my 13-year-old brother Bob said, "Stop hitting your leg like that." I quit drumming and stared out the window. I felt frustrated by the whole weekend and did what I always did—buried my feelings, knowing that everything would be *Just Fine*. And besides, the next morning at 7, two-a-day football practices were to start at the high school.

13
A DIVORCED TEENAGER
STUDIES FOR THE MINISTRY

By late in the summer of 1974, I had made two trips across Kansas, reached out for help from a Methodist minister who sent me to look for girls in the campus bars, and memorized popular songs while sitting on the roof. Then Mom called. Classes were about to begin, and she caught me totally off guard. "Before you get into all these classes this fall, have you thought about whether studying for the ministry is something you really should do? One of my friends told me she doesn't think a church would ever hire someone to be their minister if he has been divorced."

I held the phone against my ear, saying nothing.

Mom said, "Hello? Are you still there?"

"Yeah, Mom. I am here. I'm really not sure what you're saying."

"I love you, but I just think you need to think long and hard about studying for the ministry, given your circumstances." Raising my voice, I said, "Mom, okay. But why call me now? I know all about what you are saying." In fact, I knew nothing about what she was saying. I had no idea how a pastor was even hired, not to mention one who had been divorced. In fact, I knew very few pastors and not anyone who had been divorced.

Mom said that I should talk with the elders back at my home church, asking them what they thought about what I should do. "That's fine, Mom," I said, "except not one of them has ever mentioned it. Besides, they voted to have the church pay my entire tuition, as they are with the other kids in our church who are studying for the ministry at the college. How much more of an endorsement can a guy get? So no, I am not going to speak with them about what I should do."

For a guy who was pretty disconnected with his emotions and always *Just Fine*, that night, at least for the moment, I was connected. I surprised even myself. In fact, I was terribly afraid about what was ahead.

"Mom, I am 19 years old. A few weeks ago I signed divorce papers. I am about to jump headlong into studying for the ministry. I don't even know how the people here feel or think about divorce. But at this point I have picked out my classes for the semester. We will see where it goes from here. That is all I know."

She softened her voice. "Honey, I am praying for you."

"Thank you, Mom. I appreciate that. I need your prayers. At this point, how could I know what the future holds?"

"Whatever happens, you will do very well. You always do. You know I love you."

"Well, okay Mom, I appreciate that. Thanks for calling." After I hung up, I kicked a yellow bean bag chair across the floor and yelled, "Thanks for making my day, Mom. You really know how to make your son feel like a million bucks. And by the way, I do not always do well. Look at the last year of my life."

———

Just days before Mom's call, I had told my summer partner on the college paint crew that my wife had filed for divorce. Just two months earlier, he had gotten married himself and talked incessantly about how wonderful it was—"If you know what I mean." But after I told him about being divorced he said, "Wow. Are you planning to still study for the ministry?"

"What do you mean?"

"I'm just wondering. That's all."

I thought, "No you are aren't. Say what you're really thinking—that a divorced person should not be studying for the ministry." If I had only lived with my girlfriend and broken up instead of getting married and divorced, I wouldn't be questioned. He would have found that a dramatic line in my testimony. But I didn't say any of that. Instead, I answered straight up. "My plan is to study for the ministry." Afterward, I wished I had not said anything. The rest of the afternoon I was quiet, although I did swear a blue streak under my breath—mostly cursing at myself for having ever told him I was divorced. When we cleaned our brushes at the end of the day, he asked, "Are you okay? You haven't said a word for the last two hours."

"Of course," I said, calmly. "I'm *Just Fine*." That is, I thought, if you can be fine when you feel totally judged. Little did I know that the judgment was about to really ramp up.

———

One of my classes that year was called *The Life of Christ*. It was an overview of the four Gospels. Sometime in October we reached the place where Jesus talks about divorce. Sitting in the back row of a class of 50 students, I remembered Mom's conversation before classes had begun and thought, "Oh boy, here it comes." Dr. Leach, the New Testament professor, talked about men in the Old Testament who granted their wives certificates of divorce. Then he read Jesus' words directly from Matthew 19.

> *8 Jesus replied, "Moses permitted you to divorce your wives because your hearts were hard. But it was not this way from the beginning. 9 I tell you that anyone who divorces his wife, except for sexual immorality, and marries another woman commits adultery."*

There didn't seem any wiggle room there. I was surprised, and frankly, the words seemed incredibly harsh. I thought, "Boy, I don't know about this Jesus. He's strict." Choosing his words carefully, the professor said those who have been divorced "may not be the best candidates for the ministry." That surprised me, too. My heart dropped as I had a feeling of resignation that I was probably in the wrong place. Because there were only a few hundred students at the college, I figured Dr. Leach probably knew about my divorce, but I never had spoken with him in person, other than to exchange pleasantries.

"May not be the best candidates?" I thought, "Or cannot be candidates at all?" Walking back to my apartment, I said out loud, "Well, which is it?" Especially confusing was something I had heard him say previously about those he felt should enter the ministry. He said that a gifted electrician, even one with marginal people skills, should still strongly consider becoming a pastor and perhaps not an electrician. "The need is that great." That confused me and did not sit well with me. Don't we need electricians?

Back in my apartment I fantasized about what I might I have done. What if I had stood up in the class and said, "Ah, excuse me, but I've been divorced. Which is it? Can I be a pastor or not? By the way, it is why I am here and what I am preparing to do." Sitting on my couch and rereading Jesus' words where he says a person cannot be divorced except for sexual immorality, I was even more perplexed. And besides, that was not my issue. The cause of my divorce was teenage immaturity.

14
HIDING

I n that same *Life of Christ* class, I became friends with a girl who took her classes seriously. She knew I was rebuilding my life and saw that I really was trying to learn as much as I could. Not long after the class began, we admitted to each other that neither of us had ever even read the Gospels before signing up for the class. Our desire to learn more drew us toward each other, and I felt like she never judged me. Our textbook was *The Christ of the Gospels—An Exegetical Study*, written by J.W. Shephard. The author was a good writer, and I liked the way he brought the gospels alive for me. One day we reached the section in Luke 4 where the religious officials in Nazareth, Jesus' home town, were so furious with Jesus' teaching they wanted to kill him. Luke describes what happened.

All the people in the synagogue were furious when they heard this. They got up, drove him out of the town, and took him to the brow of the hill on which the town was built, in order to throw him off the cliff. But he walked right through the crowd and went on his way. Luke 4:28-30

Shephard said the Jewish officials tried to throw Jesus off a *precipice*. My friend ran into me on campus and asked me what precipice meant. I had not done the reading for the day but immediately made up an answer, saying, "It's another word for people."

"Really?" she asked. "That doesn't fit the context."

"Could be," I said. "That's what it means." She shrugged and walked away. I said to myself, "Don, why are you being so ridiculous?"

Later that evening she looked me up and said, "Hey Mister-it's-another-word-for-people. Precipice means a steep cliff." She had her finger in the spot where Shephard used the word and had me read it. Obviously, she was correct, and I looked foolish. Totally embarrassed, I said, "I'm sorry. I should not have *did* that to you."

"You mean you should not have *done* that to me," she said, correcting my grammar. "You're forgiven. You just have to be honest." That night I went back to my apartment, put on my kick-me sign and called myself "a stupid divorced kid from northwestern Kansas." But first thing the next morning, I drove to the office of the *Manhattan Mercury*—the daily paper—and subscribed. Each morning the paper was delivered to the porch of my apartment house. Reading it cover to cover became part of my self-assigned homework each day. Columnists Jack Anderson, Russell Baker, and Mary McGrory became my teachers. I especially liked Mary McGrory. She was sassy and a wordsmith. Sometimes I stood in my living room and read McGrory's columns out loud. If I didn't know a particular word, which was often, I looked it up in my dictionary, wrote the definition on a three by five notecard, and used the word in a sentence—words like *precipice*. I also liked carrying the paper around all day. Taking my paper with me meant I always had a convenient way to hide if I didn't want to talk with people. The fact that I was studying at a very conservative Christian college never was far from my mind and burying my head in my paper was convenient more than once.

That summer I returned to Colby and got a job painting natural gas meters, most of which were clear at the back of houses next to the alley. I let my hair and beard grow. Grandma Jennings called me Moses. I spent my days driving a pickup through alleys with a can of gray paint and a paint brush. In the evening I sat on the front porch reading the *Denver Post*. Since my divorce was only a year removed, I didn't want to see anybody in my hometown, and I pretty-much succeeded. Lowering the *Denver Post* from my face one evening, I told my dad that I liked Jimmy Carter. He had declared his candidacy for the 1976 Democratic presidential nomination the previous December. When I told Dad, a life-long Republican, that Carter said he would never lie to the American people, Dad harumphed and said, "That's what they all say." The 1976 presidential election was the first time I could vote, and I cast my vote for Carter. Dad later asked me, "Why did you do that?"

"I thought Carter was the better man, Dad." Although I voted for Carter a second time, Ronald Reagan trounced Carter in the 1980 election.

While the daily paper became my friend, it also added to my tension, making me realize how much I didn't know. When I got back to Manhattan in August, I started back up reading the Manhattan paper. One day the paper featured an article about the changing view of America toward divorce. That immediately caught the attention of a divorced kid studying for the ministry. If views were changing, as the article suggested, I didn't see hints of that in my neck of the woods.

Abortion became legal in the United States in 1973, and I read every piece in the paper that mentioned abortion. I even talked with a sweet girl who had an abortion. That evening in the college library, I read an article in a magazine about how there was no real consensus even among the Southern Baptist seminary professors and seminarians on their views about abortion. The newspaper helped me understand that there are disagreements on every issue.

15
NOT CALLED TO THAT CHURCH

In September 1975 several of us gathered in a friend's apartment for haircuts. I hadn't cut my hair or trimmed my beard for 14 months, ever since returning from Colby with fresh divorce papers in hand. After signing those papers, all I wanted to do was hide, and I found the perfect way to do it—behind my red beard and hair that grew down to my shoulders. I wore blue jeans, a flannel shirt and a navy stocking cap.

Just weeks after mounds of hair had fallen on that tiled kitchen floor, one of my classmates approached me, asking me if I would be interested in preaching at a church in rural Barnes, 50 miles northwest of Manhattan. He was among the students at the college who served as weekend preachers at small churches in the area. He was too busy to maintain his weekend jaunt. The 100-mile round trip included spending Saturday evening with a retired couple in the church, preaching on Sunday and having lunch with a church family before heading back to Manhattan. He thought I'd be a good choice to take his place. Would I at least make a visit to church, and just explore it? "I love the people," he said. "Are you willing to give it a shot?"

Laughing, I told him the only time I had ever preached was a 6-minute sermon when I was 15. That semester I was in a preaching class with wannabe preachers. At that point in the semester, I had spoken just once. The only comment I remember from one of the critique sheets was, "I think you need to work on your preacher's voice." I guess he thought I should yell.

"Your lack of experience doesn't matter," my friend insisted. "They won't hold that against you. How are you going to learn to preach if you don't preach in a real-life setting?" The more I hemmed and hawed, the more he pressed. "These are the sweetest people on planet earth. You'll love them; they'll love you. The couple where I stay every week already has told me you can stay with them. Don't worry about any kind of major sermon preparation." Because we were both taking the class on I John, he said, "Just look through your notes and find something you like. Then just preach from your notes and tell them a little about why you're here at college studying for the ministry. That's it—period. I will even help you prepare what you want to say, if you'd like."

Finally I said, "Well, okay. I'll do it." By Friday, though, I almost reneged. Saturday morning I spent two hours in the library scouring my notes from the class on I John, writing out a few thoughts and then throwing them into the waste basket. Finally I settled on some notes from class and decided to take my entire 3-ring notebook up to the pulpit when I spoke. Just in case I needed it, I thought. Late that afternoon, feeling nervous and uncertain, I drove up to Barnes, a community of 200 people. The couple who invited me to stay with them were out on their front porch, waiting to greet me. They were as sweet as pie. That evening we actually had pie and ice cream.

They asked me to tell them my story, especially how I ended up at a Christian college studying for the ministry. To my surprise, before I knew it I was telling them about my marriage and divorce. Some of the students knew I was divorced, but I never had spoken with anyone about it—certainly not like this. If it came up at all, I was vague and quickly moved the conversation to another topic. But that night, the couple gave me their undivided attention and I relaxed, telling them the full story and even asking them for their wisdom.

When I finished, the wife spoke up and said, "I am so sorry." She gave me a hug and said, "Let's hold hands and pray." As the three of us stood in the living room holding hands, she nodded to her husband, who prayed, asking God to bless me, "in spite of his many challenges." The next morning, I walked up to the pulpit with my Bible and the black 3-ring binder. The pulpit was too small to hold them both and I fought to balance them. After the service, I stood at the back of the church shaking hands with people. One fellow said, "You were having a hard time manhandling your notebook, weren't you?" The couple I stayed with walked me to my car. While the wife handed me a paper bag lunch with a can of Coke at the bottom of the bag, her husband pressed a $30 check into the palm of my hand. It was the first time I had been paid to speak at a church. On the drive back to Manhattan, I thought about what it might mean for me to be a pastor. I actually thought I might like it.

That afternoon I looked up my friend and said, "Hey, it went well. I am open to serving in the church, if they want me." He was thrilled and said, "I knew you would like them. The elders have a meeting tonight. They all are great guys. They will be calling me." While I didn't see him on Monday, he found me after I left my last class on Tuesday and said, "I need to chat with you for a second."

"What's up?" I asked.

"I got a call last night from the chairman of the elders. He said he had talked with the couple where you stayed this weekend. They said you told them your story."

"That's right. They wanted to know more about me."

"I'm not sure how to say this, but they are not interested in having you back."

"Really?"

Shuffling back and forth, he said, "I'm afraid so."

"Gee, what happened?"

"The chairman told me that they were divided on whether they should invite you because you have been divorced."

"No kidding. Wow."

"I'm sorry I pushed you so hard to go there. I did not anticipate this happening."

"Thanks for telling me," I shrugged. "Oh well. That's life."

———

Back at my apartment, I sat on the couch and stared at the wall thinking, "It may have been life, but was it God?" What was it my friend did not anticipate? A confused 20-year-old kid telling an 80-year-old couple that he already had been married and divorced? The couple telling the church elders that I had been divorced? Or the elders of the church deciding that anyone who had ever been divorced would not be a good candidate to serve their church?

The rejection hit me hard. I hung a "Kick Me" sign around my neck and beat myself up. "Who in the world do you think you are studying at this Christian college, you stupid Follis kid? You are a divorced boy from Northwestern Kansas—obviously in the wrong place, studying the wrong thing."

Occasionally I had seen self-hatred in my family line but didn't know what to call it. In his frustration, Dad sometimes would say, "One of these days we Follises will be dead and gone and no one will have to mess with us." That confused me, but that afternoon, sadly, I was Exhibit A. Writer Henri Nouwen says that self-rejection is the greatest enemy of the spiritual life because it contradicts the sacred voice that calls us the *beloved*. I felt anything but beloved after being told that rural church did not want me. But circumstances can change and they did for me. A decade later I was a campus pastor at the University of Illinois when I heard the word beloved. One afternoon I was praying in St. John's Catholic Chapel. As I focused on the crucifix hanging high above the altar, I felt God say, "You are my son Don Follis—my boy, *my beloved*."

"Your *beloved*?" Surely I had gotten that wrong.

"Yes, my *beloved* son." Tears fell from eyes. Never had I thought of myself as God's *beloved*.

But that afternoon after being told the church didn't want me, I felt totally rejected and uncertain about my future. After verbally pummeling myself until I was exhausted, I walked to a fish and chips place near campus. The song *Brandy (You're a fine girl)* by the group *Looking Glass* played on the juke box. Brandy was a fine girl, but I did not feel like a fine boy that day. When I paid my tab, Tony Orlando and Dawn sang *Tie a Yellow Ribbon Round the Ole Oak Tree*. The first lines grabbed me.

I'm coming home.
I've done my time. Now I've got to know what is
and isn't mine.
If you received my letter telling you I'd soon be free,
then you'll know just what to do,
if you still want me.

I was studying for the ministry and suddenly feeling that I had prison time yet to serve. Could it be possible that might mean relinquishing the idea of becoming a pastor? Was Mom's friend right that ministry as a vocation was the wrong pursuit for me? I was confused, puzzled to no end. But as I walked slowly back to my apartment, I felt the Lord spoke to my heart, saying, "You don't have to serve any time, Don. I've already served your time for you. I love you. Don't worry. We're going to get this figured out."

The next morning I felt I had to get some resolution to what had happened. Without hesitation, I walked into the college president's office and asked his secretary if I could have five minutes of the president's time later that day.

"How about 15 minutes at 4:30?" she said.

"I'll be here."

At 4:30, President Bill Lown's secretary ushered me into his office. Stepping from behind his desk, he sat down beside me in one of the two chairs facing his desk.

"What brings you here this fine afternoon, Mr. Follis?" he asked. The 55-year-old president was slim and wore glasses. His gray hair was well trimmed, as was his close-cropped mustache. He wore a navy suit, white shirt, and tie. With a smile on his face, he said, "I miss your long hair and beard." Smiling back, I cut to the chase. "Thank you for your time, sir. I want to tell you about something that happened this past weekend that left me pretty confused."

Before I had enrolled in classes a year earlier, he had invited me to his home one evening, asking about my divorce and giving me his blessing to be a student in good standing. That afternoon, I proceeded to tell him what happened at the church in Barnes, finally asking point blank, "If a person who has been divorced cannot be a pastor, am I at the wrong school, preparing for the wrong vocation?" He listened carefully as I said, "If the Bible says a divorced person can't be a pastor—as a lot of churches seem to think and perhaps many of the professors here may as well—then I'll just finish out the semester and move on. I'm just 20. I'm sure that I have a lot of things to figure out." Though my voice was calm, even saying that made me realize that the stakes were high. Reaching over and placing his hand on my forearm, President Lown spoke quietly. "Don, thank you for coming to my office. That took courage. I am sorry the news from the Barnes church came back so dismissively. I wish they would have communicated directly with you. I am sorry they didn't."

"That's what I think they should have done, too," I said, shaking my head.

Looking right at me, he said, "I am glad you are here studying. You're welcome to stay. I hope you do. I think some churches within the Christian Church/Church of Christ movement may be a bit more understanding about divorce than they have been in previous generations. But sadly, not much. I won't lie to you. What that will mean for your future, I'll be honest—I don't pretend to know." We sat and talked for another 30 minutes. Feeling that I had been heard and my feelings validated in what I said, I didn't ask him what my professors thought about the issue. I don't think I really wanted to know, given what he had just said. Though I decided to stay at the school, I was not settled. I thought of my home church paying my entire tuition to study for the ministry. I sure wasn't going to tell them about the Barnes church rejection.

Back in my apartment I grabbed my Bible and reread the words of Jesus in Matthew 19, where he speaks about divorce.

3 Some Pharisees came to him to test him. They asked, "Is it lawful for a man to divorce his wife for any and every reason?"

4 "Haven't you read," he replied, "that at the beginning the Creator 'made them male and female,' 5 and said, 'For this reason a man will leave his Father and Mother and be united to his wife, and the two will become one flesh'? 6 So they are no longer two, but one flesh. Therefore what God has joined together, let no one separate."

7 "Why then," they asked, "did Moses command that a man give his wife a certificate of divorce and send her away?"

8 Jesus replied, "Moses permitted you to divorce your wives because your hearts were hard. But it was not this way from the beginning. 9 I tell you that anyone who divorces his wife, except for sexual immorality, and marries another woman commits adultery."

10 The disciples said to him, "If this is the situation between a husband and wife, it is better not to marry."

11 Jesus replied, "Not everyone can accept this word, but only those to whom it has been given. 12 For there are eunuchs who were born that way, and there are eunuchs who have been made eunuchs by others—and there are those who choose to live like eunuchs for the sake of the kingdom of heaven. The one who can accept this should accept it." Matthew 19:3-12.

Laying my Bible down, I didn't know what to think. I was grateful for President Lown's kindness but frustrated and confused at being rejected by the church.

Over the decades, I have known all kinds of people who are

divorced for reasons other than sexual immorality. There had been no sexual immorality in my youthful marriage. Most of the people I know who are divorced eventually got remarried, as did I. As did my first wife. I prayed that she would. Moses permitted men to divorce their wives, but I thought of the countless women whose lives were destroyed by that law at a time when they had no legal rights themselves. I came to believe that though God never intends for anyone to be divorced, God forgives all kinds of sins—all the time. That is the heart of the Christian faith. So often in trying to decide who is in and who is out, we somehow think we can manage or control God's love and forgiveness. That's just not our job. God is faithful and unrelenting in his love. "If we confess our sins, "he is faithful and just and will forgive us our sins and purify us from all unrighteousness." (I John 1:9.) Even the Apostle Paul— a stellar Jew, an outstanding Pharisee if ever there was one— wrote to the church in Philippi admitting he did not understand the message of the cross of Jesus until God brought him to his knees and explained the power of second chances.

———

Early in my campus ministry days when Jennifer and I were newly married, I met a woman working at the University of Illinois who had intractable views about remarriage. She was a serious Christian, as was her husband, at least as she told it. Still, he had left her for another woman. "I hope you get a chance to remarry one day," I said.

"Oh, that won't happen,"

"Why do you say that?"

"Read Matthew 19," she said flatly. One day sitting in a coffee shop we actually read it together. No matter what I said, she did not budge, insisting that she could never remarry. "But he left you," I said. When I pressed her to be open to remarriage, she finally closed her Bible and said, "This conversation is frustrating me. I am not changing my mind." She stood up and walked off. As she headed back to her campus office, I thought back to that day after I talked with the college president about being rejected. I still remember my prayer after reading Matthew 19 many times that afternoon: "Lord, you got anything for a teenager who simply blew it and is wondering what in the world it means to try and put his life back together?"

16

SAYING ALL THE PRAYERS

After being rejected by the church in Barnes, I isolated myself from the other students even more than I already had. I was lonely most of the time but I didn't want to be rejected again. Not only had I been rejected by a wife, now a church had rejected me. Still, most students didn't know much about what happened to me, which is the way I wanted it. Besides my older sister who loved me and hung with me, there was another student at the college who kept reaching out to me. He was John Messer, a fellow from rural southwest Kansas who was already married when we met. John and his wife, Marcia, welcomed me to their apartment. We became fast friends. Their friendship was salve to my soul. In the evening John and I talked and drank coffee in his apartment. When I married Jennifer in Phoenix in 1978, John was my best man.

A few months after the Barnes church incident, John told me he was moving on from preaching in a tiny church in Westmoreland. "They would be glad to have you," he said. "Especially if you want to work on your preaching. It's just a 25-mile drive from Manhattan. Interested?" Though I wavered—especially with the memory of the Barnes church fresh in my mind —I finally said, "Sure, why not." John made a phone call, came over to my apartment and told me, "Harold the Elder said to come on over this Sunday."

"Harold the Elder?"

"Well, he's the only man. I call him Harold the Elder."

"The only man."

"It's a tiny group. There are about 10 people—eight or nine older women and Harold and his wife."

"Ten people. That's it?"

"That's right. Why not just go and try it."

I threw caution to the wind. The first Sunday when I drove up to a traditional white building with a steeple on top, there were no cars in the gravel lot. When I tried the wooden door, it was locked. Just then a car pulled into the lot and a man about 60 stepped out. "Hello. I'm Harold." He said. "You must be Don."

"Hi. Yes, I am Don Follis."

"Thanks for coming. Do you like to preach?"

"Sure." I didn't tell him I had preached only twice.

"We keep her open to give some of the boys from the Christian college a chance to preach." While we stood on the sidewalk, Harold told me about the order of service. "You are the preacher. You say the prayers. I am a man of faith, but I don't pray in public. Are you okay with that?"

"Yes, I am okay with that."

Harold unlocked and pulled open the creaky door. I wore a brown plaid leisure suit, a green tie and a white belt. Harold wore his gray suit with a blue tie. The building smelled musty. It was only opened on Sunday. There was a bathroom but no water. If you needed a bathroom you went next door, where one of the members lived. On one wall of the musty church hung two pictures of Jesus—one of Jesus praying in the Garden of Gethsemane and the other of Jesus standing on a green hillside with a lamb draped over his shoulders. I often wondered where every church in America got those pictures. In the sanctuary, two rows of ten wooden pews lined the brown tile aisle. A wobbly wooden lectern humbly commanded the middle of a small stage. An American flag stood on one side of the stage; a Christian flag stood on the other. Beside the stage, an old upright piano had seen better days.

Sure enough, within a few minutes ten women had shown up. One woman escorted two grade-school-age granddaughters, one on each hand. Several ladies walked to church from nearby homes. A woman walked to the piano and started playing. Church had started. Without any welcome or introduction, we sang *What a Friend We have in Jesus* and *The Old Rugged Cross*. Then Harold stood and read from I Corinthians 11, saying, "Whenever you eat this bread and drink this cup, you proclaim the Lord's death until he comes again." He passed a tray of juice and small white wafers that his wife had brought in from the car.

"Today, we have Don Follis here to preach," Harold said, following the communion service. "Let's welcome him." The ladies clapped and I carried my Bible to the rickety pulpit. After I spoke for 10 minutes, we sang a song. Harold gave me a nod and I gave a benediction. Pointing with his index finger to the door, he gave another nod, and I moved to the door. Everyone shook my hand but quickly left. Harold shut off the lights and stood by the wooden door with the key jingling in his hand. He handed me a check for $30. When I opened my car door, Harold said, "See you next Sunday." By the first Sunday in December, I had preached six times and had begun chatting a few minutes with the ladies following the service. Leading up to Christmas, I decided to try some Christmas sermons. When

I began the first one, I noticed that the woman who brought her grade-school-age granddaughters was watching them color Christmas trees from coloring books. The grandmother sat on the front row, while her granddaughters were on their bellies in front of the pew, just beneath the stage where I was preaching. Crayons rolled all over the floor. Every part of me wanted to scream, "For crying out loud, I'm a confused young kid studying for the ministry and trying to figure out life. Would you please quit coloring on your stomachs right in front of the pulpit."

The coloring granddaughters became the main show of the morning. The grandmother talked to the children in loud whispers. After a couple of minutes, the volume of the whispering was so annoying I stopped preaching altogether. All 10 women and Harold the Elder were watching the children color. I kept preaching but gave up after another couple of minutes and said, "Well, it's been nice being with you all." Wishing them a good week, I introduced a final song—*Joy to the World*. And what a joyous morning it was. After giving the benediction I decided not to stand around and talk with the ladies, as I had been doing in previous weeks. Instead, I told Harold I needed to get back to Manhattan. I headed to my car.

"Everything okay?" he asked.

"Everything is *Just Fine*, Harold."

"Well, okay then. Thanks for coming. See you next week."

Driving back, I was mad—mad enough to say a few choice words when I pulled away from the church. But then I started to laugh because I remembered what a friend told me his pastor had once said. "I'm a good pastor until I get really mad. Then I start cussing." Well, that was true of me that Sunday. At least my swearing gave me a good laugh. I was mad for having told my friend John that I would come to the church and preach, mad at the church for not listening, mad at the church in Barnes for rejecting me, and mad that I did not have a clue about what I was going to do with my life. I felt that I was aimlessly grasping at straws. The madder I got, the faster I drove. When I was two miles outside of Manhattan, lights from a Kansas Highway Patrol car appeared in my rearview mirror. "You've got to be kidding me," I said, hitting the steering wheel with my hand. When the trooper walked up to my car, he asked me what my hurry was. "I am a student at the Christian college in Manhattan. I've been preaching in a little town and am in a hurry to get back so I can study this afternoon."

"Preacher," he said, "I don't care how big a hurry you are in, you can't drive this fast out on these little highways. You were going at least 70."

"Seventy?"

"Or faster. The speed limit right here is 50. I was going almost 70 when you passed me."

"I passed you?"

"Yes sir."

"I'm so sorry, sir."

He handed me a speeding ticket and said, "You keep on preaching, preacher. But slow her down when you get on the road after church." I laid the $45 speeding ticket on the passenger's side of the bench seat next to the $30 check Harold had written me that morning. By the time I pulled up into my apartment parking lot, I was so frustrated that I called Harold and told him I would not be back. "Harold, I've been thinking about it and have decided to make my sermon today my last. I know I am putting you in a bind. I'm sorry."

"What happened?"

"Nothing, Harold. I'm just not a good fit."

"Would you give me two more weeks, please? That would take us up to Christmas."

"Well okay, Harold," I relented. "I'll give you two more

weeks." On my last Sunday, Harold's wife brought Christmas cookies. Driving back to Manhattan, I ate the entire plate of cookies and drove 50 mph.

————

When I got back to my apartment, I took a walk instead of studying for my last final. After meandering through the K-State campus, I ended up at St. Isidore's Catholic Student Center. Almost every afternoon when I went for a jog I went past St. Isidore's but I never had entered. That Sunday afternoon I pushed on the door and found it unlocked. Inside, students were studying, playing ping-pong and drinking hot chocolate. A couple of students said "hello" as I walked over to where newspapers and magazines were stacked. Near the magazines I noticed a framed copy of the Apostles' Creed hanging on the wall. I read it.

"I believe in God the Father Almighty, creator of heaven and earth; I believe in Jesus Christ His only Son our Lord. He was conceived by the Holy Spirit and born of the Virgin Mary. He suffered under Pontius Pilate, was crucified, died and was buried. He descended to the dead. On the third day he rose again. He ascended into heaven and is seated at the right hand of the Father. He will come again to judge the living and the dead.

"I believe in the Holy Spirit, the holy catholic church, the communion of saints, the forgiveness of sins, the resurrection of the body and the life everlasting."

As I pondered the creed, a girl walked up to me and asked me if I knew it. "I am not familiar with it," I said. "But it is beautiful."

"We pray it at Mass every week." She was a K-State

student. "I pray it in my dorm room in the morning, too. It is a good way to begin the day."

"That's wonderful."

"You are welcome to come by St. Isidore's any time."

Neither the Christian college nor its sponsoring churches—the Christian Churches and Churches of Christ that I grew up in—prayed the creeds. We didn't have websites then, but if we did, it would have read as the current website now explains:

> *Manhattan Christian College pleads for the unity of all believers on the common ground of commitment and obedience to the lordship of Christ. Believing that creeds of men, however correct, perpetuate sectarianism and create division within the church when made tests of fellowship, we have no creed except faith in Jesus as the Christ, God's Son and humankind's Savior.*

I knew almost nothing about the creeds, let alone what might perpetuate sectarianism and create division within the church. All I knew was that I was drawn to the Apostles' Creed. I ran every afternoon—both for exercise and to pound out my stress. From then on during those jogs, I often stepped into St. Isidore's, stood directly in front of the creed and prayed it. The Apostles' Creed would become a central part of my walk with God.

PART THREE
PEERING INTO THE FUTURE

17
ASKING GOOD QUESTIONS

When I told my adult daughter Maddie about my confusion and uncertainty after my experiences at the churches in Barnes and Westmoreland, she was puzzled. "Then why did you stick around that college, studying for the ministry? Why didn't you just go on to something totally different?"

I told her I had no idea what I wanted to do and was so deeply rooted in the *Land of Numb*, I didn't know what direction to turn, so I just stayed at the school. I couldn't imagine my options. I had said at church camp that I wanted to be a minister but now I was far from certain. Mostly I felt discouraged and lonely. I remembered the Methodist minister telling me to move on with my life when I sought his counsel. I really had no idea what I wanted to do, but as I pondered Maddie's question, I came up with an answer. I remembered the events of the spring of 1976.

Early in the semester, the college president, Bill Lown, saw me in the hallway and asked me if I would ride with him that coming Sunday to a church where he was slated to preach and talk about the college. I nervously accepted his invitation, wondering why he had asked me. He had been nice to me on two significant occasions—once when I first met him in his home in 1974 when I told him about my divorce and again when I met with him in his office after the church in Barnes rejected me. While I didn't know him very well, I was taken with his sincerity and warmth.

We met in the college parking lot at 6:30 a.m. for a two-hour drive. The entire trip, President Lown held court, telling me his life story, which I knew nothing about. He was a good storyteller and I peppered him with questions. As we headed back that afternoon, President Lown turned the conversation toward me. After I told him about my growing up years, he got right down to where the tire hits the road, asking me what it was like studying for the ministry after being divorced. He knew what happened to me with the church in Barnes, but neither he nor anyone had asked me that question in such a pointed way. I told him the truth, saying that I liked my classes but thinking about the future felt scary and uncertain.

"What part feels uncertain?" he asked.

"Even though I am studying to enter the ministry, I just don't know what I'll end up doing or who will even accept me."

"That must feel scary," he said.

"It sure does."

———

When I started counseling and mentoring pastors full time in 2010, I realized that *what* questions are the best questions you can ask. That's what Bill Lown had done with me that day decades before. I've never forgotten it, and I use *what* questions every day in my ministry with pastors. They get right down to the real issues. What are your options? What do think God is saying to you in this? What is next? Whether it was his asking me questions like those, or the way he listened as we drove, he made me feel accepted and important. Having now counseled many pastors, I know that those who feel listened to, feel loved. They can hardly tell the difference. President Lown was perhaps the first person ever to listen to me so well and to ask me good questions. I felt loved.

———

As we pulled into Manhattan, President Lown smiled and completely surprised me by asking, "I bet you'd like to get married again. Wouldn't you?"

I didn't see that question coming. "I sure would, President Lown." Suddenly I felt that I had said the wrong thing by being so quick with my answer. I didn't say anything and waited for his response, which for some reason I thought would be painful to hear. But it was the exact opposite.

"I can't blame you. I love being married. Do you mind if my wife and I pray that God will lead you to a wife who is perfect for you?"

Realizing I was on safe ground after all, I said, "I would love that, President Lown."

When we pulled into the school parking lot he asked, "May I pray for you before you get out of the car?"

"Sure."

Resting his hand on my shoulder, he asked God to bless my studies and lead me to both a ministry and a wife that would be just right for me. After he said amen, he shook my hand. "I think you're at the right place. I am really glad you are here. And by the way, you are a good conversationalist, too."

When I stepped out of the car, I felt relieved. I believed God loved me enough to give me another chance. I always wondered if it felt risky for President Lown to pray that I would find a good ministry and a good wife. Surely he knew that most of the churches that financially supported the college would not hire a minister who had been divorced. I never told anyone about the conversation that day. Until now, that is. Bill and Nadine Lown can look down from heaven, knowing their prayers for me were answered.

A few weeks later I traveled with President Lown again. We went with one of the singing groups from the school and all traveled in a 15-passenger van. The school president preached at the church in the morning, and the singing group gave an evening concert. On the way home, President Lown engaged a student named Tom who was trying to figure out what he would do with his life—continue studying for the ministry or get a business degree from K-State. I listened as President Lown worked his magic, asking Tom several questions. What led you to this college? What kinds of things bring you joy? What are you really good at? What do you think your options are? Deep down, what do you really want to do? What do you think God is saying to you? A week later, Tom told me he would pursue a business degree full time at Kansas State and drop out of the ministerial program. "Boy, did President Lown ask me great questions."

———

Not long after that second trip, I found out that a public relations job was opening up at the college—a job that required travel, presenting the college in churches, and recruiting students. I thought it might be a good way for me to step into my future, whatever it might be. Late one afternoon while I was jogging, I saw President Lown walking to his car. I took the chance to ask him about the job. The position was advertised to start in May and required being on the road for 11 weeks that summer. Because I had taken extra classes, I needed only 12 hours to graduate by the following May. If he were open to it, I thought I could work the PR job and spread my remaining classes over two semesters. "I think I might be a good fit. Would you consider me?" He said he would keep me in mind. After a few days I figured nothing would come of it and wondered what I might do next. I was planning to return to my hometown and work for the summer when I got a note in my student mailbox from the president's secretary, saying that President Lown wanted to speak with me. In his office the next day, he said, "I've been thinking about your interest in the job. Taking your hours over the course of the entire year is not a problem."

But there was something more important, he said. "This is a job that requires a lot of trust between me, the school's development office, churches throughout the Midwest, and you. You would represent the school, speak in lots of churches and homes, give congregations updates on the college, and thank them for their financial partnership." Pausing and looking straight at me, he asked, "Do you think you can learn to do that?"

"I will do my best. I think I can learn it."

"Does it excite you?"

"Completely."

"What you say about the school, or me, or our faculty, very likely will be repeated. That's my hope, of course."

"I understand that, sir."

"How you look is important. People make an initial judgment the first time they meet us."

"I understand that. First impressions are crucial."

Smiling, he said, "By the way, I liked your long hair and

beard that you had last year. With your navy stocking cap and blue jeans, it was a pretty good look."

"Don't worry. I won't be growing it back any time soon."

"You've heard me speak, so you can probably guess that proper grammar is important to me. It's not just what you say. It's how you say it. I know that takes practice, but if you work hard at it, you can probably get really good at it."

"I'd like to get good at it. I'm willing to work hard to sharpen my skills."

"I think you do want that. I can tell." The two of us had talked for hours previously. He seemed to like me. "You come across as a genuine, friendly person. I do not hold that divorce against you." That's the first time I ever heard that.

"Thank you, sir. That means a lot to me."

"So I'll keep it short. I'd like to offer you the job."

My heart jumped. "Thank you. Wow. I am surprised. In a good way, I mean. This means so much to me."

"What do you think?" he asked.

"I don't know what to say. I accept. I will do my best." Standing up, he shook my hand and said, "Welcome aboard, Don Follis. Now get yourself over to the development office and get things set up for yourself. I'll tell them you are coming." At the development office, I said, "President Lown just offered me a job and sent me over here."

"Congratulations!" the secretary said. "He told us you were coming over." When I finished the paper work, I walked a block down to Varney's campus bookstore and purchased Dale Carnegie's *How to Win Friends and Influence People*, first copyright in 1936. In the coming weeks I wrote pages of quotations from the book on lined notebook paper and stuck them inside the back cover of my Bible. One quotation has stayed with me my whole life. "A person's name is to that person the sweetest and most important sound in any language." I wrote those words on a note card and stuck it in the front flap of my Bible.

———

And there's the answer to my daughter's question. I stayed at the college because a man I grew to respect—Bill Lown—gave gave me a chance, first by encouraging me to be a student, then by showing understanding when a church rejected me, and finally by offering me a job. Though he saw real potential, not failure, he also did not pretend that he knew what my future held. He didn't pretend that it was going to be easy for me. I respected him for that and for still taking a chance with me. I realized that he put his own reputation on the line, trusting that I could do the job, and trusting that I could navigate talking about my divorce, if it ever came up. He had won my heart and loyalty. In a just a few weeks, my road lessons began.

———

Starting in late May 1976, I traveled all over the Midwest, speaking at churches, camps and youth groups, driving 7,000 miles that summer. President Lown gave me a 3-part assignment. Develop a 1-minute elevator speech about the school, a 3-minute talk, and a 10-minute talk. Memorize all of them. After I wrote those talks, I stood in the living room of my tiny apartment and practiced them.

Because I was given a chance to prove myself, that summer is seared in my memory. All of May I spent setting up my summer schedule while finishing up my classes. In a little office in the school development building, I made 50 phone calls asking for appointments with pastors, speaking dates in churches, and invitations to join the church camp faculty during the week of high school camps. My calendar showed appointments in Wichita, Omaha, Denver, Amarillo, Albuquerque, and Phoenix. I traced my route on my new road atlas. Keys to a new Chevrolet Vega station wagon were handed me. After loading the back of the station wagon with a college display, a slide projector, and boxes of brochures, I put my road atlas in the passenger seat. With the college MasterCard in my wallet, I was about ready to launch. On a final trip back to Varney's bookstore, I bought a black briefcase. In it, I packed my Bible, a spiral bound notebook, my book on winning friends and influencing people, and a new paperback dictionary. The day before I pulled out, President Lown found me and prayed for me. "You'll do great." Handing me a book of devotions, he said, "Have your morning devotions. Work to increase your vocabulary. (I had shown him my new dictionary earlier.) And above all, have fun."

After having preached but once at a church that didn't want me back and eight times in a church of ten women and one man, I pulled out of Manhattan, heading to Wichita for an appointment with a pastor. I was nervous during the entire two-hour drive. From Wichita I drove to Parsons in far southeastern Kansas before heading back to Hutchinson in central Kansas. After Hutchinson, I stopped in Pratt to talk with a potential student before driving 75 miles to Dodge City. At just 21 years old, I was my own boss and loving it. I didn't know all that much about the school I was representing, or its theological underpinnings. I just didn't want to say anything stupid or something that would put the college, especially President Lown, or me, in jeopardy. I wrote my summer philosophy on a notecard and taped it to the console: "Be friendly, tell the truth, be interested in everyone you meet, and treat people the way you want to be treated."

Just days into my trip, I already had driven 800 miles. At

restaurants, I sat at counters and talked with truck drivers and farmers. In a spiral notebook, I kept notes on every appointment, including conversations I had with people I met at restaurants. Everyone I met I handed my business card and asked for their address. The school president said to give my card to everyone I met. "You just never know," he said.

With my new dictionary I started recording new words in my new notebook, lists that somehow got tucked away in my files for decades. When I found the lists, I saw that in June of 1976 among the words I added were *inveterate, inimitable, and inextricable.* By the end of the summer, I had recorded more than 75 new vocabulary words and their meanings. Later that summer I was talking with my sister on the phone when she said, "You don't have to use your big words when you're talking with me."

The day I pulled into Dodge City I had an evening appointment with two high school students who had expressed interest in the college. Arriving in town about noon, I checked into a motel room early and drove over to a Dodge City tourist attraction called *Boot Hill.* Made to look like an old western town, *Boot Hill* sold taffy, cowboy hats and postcards. The door in the back of the gift shop led to a "cemetery" featuring wooden headstones painted with colorful sayings. With my Canon single-lens reflex 35mm camera, I took a picture of the epitaph that made me laugh out loud. *He drank too much and loved unwisely.*

From Dodge City, I drove north to Colby, where I spent a night with my folks and did my laundry before heading out again. The next day, I drove more than 450 miles through Nebraska and up to Rapid City, South Dakota. From there I went west 40 miles into northeastern Wyoming, where I got lost trying to find the camp where I was slated to serve on the faculty that week. After meandering here and there for almost an hour, I stopped and asked directions. That week in Wyoming I was assigned a cabin with 10 high school boys. One morning I spoke 30 minutes about the college. That week there was a singing team from another Christian college in South Dakota, accompanied by a faculty member who told me he didn't think I should be at the camp. "Why would you be way out here trying to steal students from our college in South Dakota, which is just 50 miles from this camp?"

"I was invited to be here, sir," I said.

"That surprises me," he countered.

I remembered that President Lown had told me whatever I said might get back to him and so I just said, "I'm sorry you feel that way." One of the girls on the singing team from the other college overheard that conversation and followed me outside. "I am sorry he spoke to you like that." The last night, the campers stayed up late. When I stepped into the cabin, the lights were off. No one made a sound. When I slipped into my sleeping bag, I found it filled with pine cones and needles. Jumping up, I turned on the lights and said at the top of my voice, "All right you dirty rats. Very funny." The cabin erupted.

The girl in the singing group who apologized for what her professor said to me lived in Cheyenne and was heading home after camp ended. "I am spending the night in Cheyenne," I said. "Could I buy you breakfast before I leave the next morning?"

She was quick with her answer. "Oh, no, thank you. I don't think that would be right."

Driving on from Cheyenne, I spoke to a pastor in Denver before stopping in Colorado Springs, where I had dinner with two prospective students and their parents. One of the girls had an older sister who was a student at our college. I didn't know her but after I gave my 3-minute talk about the school, she took over and talked way more than I did. Both girls ended up attending the college.

The next day I headed 390 miles to Amarillo, Texas. Driving through the vast spaces of New Mexico, I felt my confidence grow. I rolled down my window and let the hot wind blow my hair. When I arrived at the church, the pastor told me he had arranged for me to spend the night at the home of one of the church elders. After I spoke to the youth group, the pastor introduced me to a 60-year-old man dressed in a summer wool suit and tie. Trim and friendly, he said he and his wife were looking forward to having me stay with them. "Just follow me," he said. Turns out, he was a Texas oil man. After pulling into his driveway, he hopped out of his car and pointed for me to park in the circle drive in front of his house. My room had a leather reading chair, an en suite bathroom, a full-length mirror and a sliding door out to the inground pool. The man told me to change into shorts and a t-shirt. He did the same, and we sat in his family room looking out on the lighted pool while we ate ice cream and talked until 11 p.m.

The oil man told me his story of growing up in the 1930s in Midland, 250 miles south of Amarillo. His Dad worked as a roughneck in the oil fields. That's what he did, too, he said, until he became "an oil man." I asked, so he told me the difference between a roughneck and an oil man. He said that a roughneck did manual labor on oil rigs, while an oil man made decisions as an executive in the company. For the past 10 years, he had owned his own oil company. Finally, the man's wife said breakfast would be at 7. "We'd love for you to eat with us. You'll stay, won't you?"

"It would be my pleasure." The next morning after I showered, I dressed in my brand new three-piece suit, the only one I owned. It was burnt-orange. With it, I wore a black long-sleeved shirt and a white and orange striped tie. My dad would have been pleased to know I packed a shoeshine kit. I pulled it out and polished my brown penny loafers. I stood in front of the full-length mirror, smiling at myself before heading down the hall toward the kitchen.

The forecast called for the temperature to exceed 100 degrees. A 287-mile trip to Albuquerque was in front of me. Any other time I would have thrown on the shorts, t-shirt and sandals I had on the previous evening. But I figured my host would be dressed in a suit, and he was. When I walked into the kitchen, he was drinking coffee and reading the newspaper in a starched white shirt and tie. His suit jacket was draped over the chair next to him.

"You're looking dapper this morning, young man."

"Thank you, sir," I said, trying to act nonchalant.

I had to drive west on Interstate 40 for 30 miles before seeing a rest area. In the restroom, I changed into the shorts, t-shirt and sandals. At a church in Albuquerque that afternoon, I still was in my t-shirt and shorts when I suddenly found myself in a discussion about End Times prophecies. The pastor there wanted to know my and the college's view of the end of the world as we know it. I hadn't the least idea of the college's view, and very little about my own. However, the preceding summer I had read Hal Lindsay's *The Late, Great Planet Earth*, a book that sold millions of copies. Lindsay examined current events in an attempt to predict what he believed would be the rapture of believers before the tribulation and the second coming of Christ, when Christ would establish a thousand-year kingdom on earth. Lindsay used scriptures from the books of Daniel, Ezekiel, and Revelation to argue that prophecy showed the world would end soon before the year 2000. My Grandma Jennings didn't agree. When I read some of Lindsay's book to her while we sat on our front porch, she said, "If you don't quit reading me that foolishness, I am going to get up and leave." This Albuquerque pastor said he was a pre-millen-nialist, which is how Lindsay described himself. "This is exactly what the scriptures teach," the pastor said emphatically. I said I was pretty sure the college did not have a position on the End Times.

He walked me outside to a detached single-car garage. Inside was a room full of food staples—flour, sugar, and cases of canned fruit and vegetables. In one corner was a twin bed and a tiny bathroom with a sink and toilet. Above the bed hung a picture of Jesus. "You ever seen anything like this?" he asked.

"No, I haven't."

"Have you read and thought much about the book of Revelation?"

"A little." I turned my body so I could see the door.

"When do you think the tribulation will come? In our lifetime?" He wasn't backing off, so I decided to mimic his language and tone. "No man knows, brother. This being our country's bicentennial year, it could be any time. Maybe even the early 1980s."

"Exactly!" he said, slapping me on the back. "When I met you I could see we were kindred spirits. So you'll probably understand why I have all these food staples. There is a day coming when my family and I are going to need these provisions."

Actually, I did not understand all the food or the little twin bed with the picture of Jesus hanging crookedly on the wall. I wanted to get out of there as quickly as possible. "No one knows the day or the hour," was my only response. "Do you need a place to stay tonight?" he asked. "You can have your own place right back here. It is here for the taking." I was glad I had booked a hotel room for the night.

From Albuquerque, I headed 140 miles northeast into the Sangre de Cristo Mountains to work at another camp. But every afternoon at that camp, I was planning for the next week. I'd been asked to give the evening Vespers talks several nights in a row at a camp in Prescott, Arizona. I was nervous. I had a free day between the two camps, so I stopped at Winslow en route to the camp. I discovered Homolovi State Park—home to Ancestral Pueblo archaeological sites on the north cusp of Winslow. Finding a shaded picnic table, I spent several hours finishing the outlines to talks that I titled "Run Toward Heaven." My text was from the book of Hebrews.

Therefore, since we are surrounded by such a great cloud of witnesses, let us throw off everything that hinders and the sin that so easily entangles. And let us run with perseverance the race marked out for us, fixing our eyes on Jesus, the pioneer and perfecter of faith. For the joy set before him he endured the cross, scorning its shame, and sat down at the right hand of the throne of God. Consider him who endured such opposition from sinners, so that you will not grow weary and lose heart. Hebrews 12: 1-3

I'd never been in that part of the U.S. and felt free as a bird soaring through the Ponderosa Pines in the Coconino National Forest. In Prescott, I launched my four days of talks from the book of Hebrews, and it went great. By the third day, campers were greeting each other with the words, "Run Toward Heaven."

———

After 11 weeks on the road, I finally returned to campus in August, ready to stay put in Manhattan for a while and to enroll in the few the remaining classes that I needed to graduate. When President Lown and I met for coffee he told me he had talked with several pastors with whom I had met. He said he also heard good things about my "Run Toward Heaven" sermons. When he hired me, he told me word would get back to him about where I was and what I said. Apparently it had. When he shook my hand, he said, "I knew you could do it. Great job. I hope you'll stay with us here at the school for a long time."

When the waitress brought the bill, I grabbed it.

———

I did stay in school and graduate with a degree in Bible Ministries. That first fall after I graduated, I continued working the public relations job and was asked to speak in one of the weekly morning chapel services. I got to choose my topic, and for reasons I don't remember, I decided to speak on Psalm 51, where David takes Bathsheba as his own and arranges the murder of her husband Uriah. The morning I spoke, I did not mention my divorce but stressed the conviction of sin David felt after being confronted by the prophet Nathan. David owned his own sin, saying, "Against you, you only, have I sinned and done what is evil in your sight." (Psalm 51:4).

I hadn't thought about that sermon for 45 years when I got a big surprise the summer of 2021, just before moving from Illinois to Phoenix. In preparation to move I spent several days going through old files. One sermon gave me a good laugh when I read a hand-written phrase, "Raise voice here for emphasis!" While I sat cross-legged on my office floor making a huge pitch pile, I found the sermon I preached the fall of 1977. I had no idea I even had it. When I read through it, I discovered several places where I said I feel God gives people lots of chances and a wide berth, especially if they own their own sin as David did in Psalm 51. I sat there feeling proud of my 22-

year-old self for doing his best to try to honestly live out the Christian life.

The only memory I have of that day in chapel is of the first person to address me following the service. After the closing prayer, the New Testament professor made a beeline to me. He was the one who said those who are divorced may not be good candidates for the ministry. "Thank you for preaching that sermon. It is a great passage, and you preached it well. That took courage. We need to hear good words like that." He was the one who had implied divorced people might not be good candidates for the ministry.

18

JENNIFER

The public relations job bolstered the self-assurance I needed when a lovely blonde student named Jennifer Earles arrived on campus in August 1977. I was immediately enamored with this beautiful girl from the *Valley of the Sun*. Her smile and self-confidence captured me. On the encouragement of her pastor, himself a graduate of Manhattan Christian College, she decided to join a half dozen other kids from her Mesa church to attend the school. Jennifer planned to take classes for a semester or a year to get more clarity on what she believed and then return to Arizona to study journalism at a state university. Once on campus, Jennifer took a part-time job working in the public relations office, where my office was located. An afternoon in mid-September, the folks in the office threw a party for her 18th birthday. Her roommate brought ice cream and cake. Giving her a Snoopy birthday card with a Lifesaver mint inside, I teased her about being so young. I was flirting, and she knew it.

Though I barely knew her, by the time I left that party, I

wanted to marry her. That night I lay on my bed and said, "What a gorgeous girl!" The president of the college had told me he and his wife would pray that I would find a wife. "Please Lord," I prayed. "Let this be the answer." A few days later, I mustered up the courage to ask Jennifer out. Even though I was four years older and working full-time, she accepted. I was friends with several girls at the college, but this was to be my first official date in three years. Jennifer and I drank chocolate-chip milkshakes at Vista Drive In. The more we talked, the more I liked her. What she remembers is that the chocolate chips got stuck in the straw. What I remember is that she had a quick wit that made me laugh.

As we talked, I didn't bring up my divorce. But it was a small school. An upper-class student from her hometown filled her in. So at our next date, Jennifer asked me about my past. From those early days till now, Jennifer always has cut to the chase, wanting clarity. There she was in 1977, already pulling me out of the *Land of Numb*. So I told her my story.

My story did not scare her. Jennifer was the youngest of six kids from a small town in central Kentucky. Her Dad and Mom were divorced. When Jennifer was in the second grade, her Mom, Lucy, took the kids to Phoenix for Christmas to see an aunt who had set her up for a blind date with an engineer from Goodyear Aerospace. In February, Lucy flew back out to Phoenix and married him. After school was out that spring, they moved to Phoenix, where Jennifer lived through high school.

———

By Christmas, Jennifer knew that I wanted to marry her. The letters we exchanged over break left no doubt about that.

However, getting married so soon was not part of Jennifer's plan. Had we not been so in love, she might not even have returned for the second semester at Manhattan. But she did, and, well, "The rest is history." To this day I still get lost in the clouds looking at my favorite picture of Jennifer, taken on Valentine's Day 1978. Wearing a gray woolen coat and standing in ankle-deep snow in the front yard of my apartment house, she is laughing as she throws her head back and kicks snow into the air. Every time I see that picture I smile and say, "That's my girl."

My love for her had only increased by early March when I met Jerry Gibson, a University of Illinois campus minister who had come to our campus to speak at a conference on spiritual enrichment. One morning over coffee, Jerry told me he would leave his campus ministry position at the end of the semester. He grabbed my arm resting on the restaurant table and said, "Don, you must apply. You would be great."

"And move to Illinois?"

"Yes, to Champaign-Urbana, 100 miles south of Chicago."

"I've never even heard of it."

"All the better," he said. "'Toto, I have a feeling we are not in Kansas anymore.' You must apply for the position."

"But I am dating a girl named Jennifer Earles and I really don't want to leave her."

"Leave her? Who said anything about leaving her? Bring her with you. Let the two become one. Start your life together in east-central Illinois."

When I told Jennifer, she said, "Apply." Jerry had given me the name and telephone number of the chairman of the campus ministry board. "Call him this evening," Jerry insisted. "Tell him we talked."

That evening I made the call. "We plan to move quickly on

DON FOLLIS

this position. Send a letter and your resume," he said. The next morning I wrote my first ever cover letter and resume and dropped them in the mail. A week later, the board chairman called and invited me to come to Illinois to interview. The day he called I was working on my 1978 summer travel schedule. But on April 27th I flew from Manhattan to Champaign-Urbana. The next day, several board members spent the morning interviewing me. As I told them my story, I told them about my divorce. A young farmer and graduate from Illinois, said, "That's not a game changer for me." My ears perked up. After a two-hour interview, the committee members encouraged me to spend the afternoon walking around campus, getting a feel for the place and asking God about whether this was ministry I'd like to pursue.

The university sits in between Urbana and Champaign. In the center of campus is a rectangular grassy space called the Quad. At 200 feet wide and 950 feet long, the Quad is crisscrossed by sidewalks making huge X's. That particular afternoon hundreds of students sat on the Quad smoking marijuana, listening to music and playing Frisbee. I soon discovered it was a special day called *Hash Wednesday*. Police officers were out in force, but the crowd was mellow. That evening the chairman of the board took me to dinner and offered me the job. He mentioned my divorce, saying only, "Thanks for telling us that. Sounds like a hard time, but you hung in there. We think you'd be a great addition to our team." When I called Jennifer and told her I had been offered the position, she was delighted and said, "Wow! Take the job." She knew I wanted badly to be a pastor. If the campus wanted me, then go.

"The board wants me to start in the middle of July."

The next day I flew back to Manhattan and that evening I

called the board chairman and accepted the job. I discovered that campus ministries were more accepting than churches about divorce, which was a relief. But what was I supposed to do about the relationship with Jennifer—this girl from the Sonoran Desert that I was in love with and didn't want to let out of my sight? After several heart-to-heart talks in the coming days, I cut to the chase: "Jennifer, please marry me this summer and move to Illinois with me. You are the woman of my dreams. You can finish college at the University of Illinois." But Jennifer was not sure. She felt more strongly about my taking the campus ministry position than she did about marrying me so soon. Her suggestion was a long-distance relationship. I suggested marriage—tomorrow! In the *Land of Numb* I have suffered plenty from indecisiveness over the years, but not that night. I begged her to marry me and to go to Illinois with me. She said she wanted to marry me but not so young. She had grown up a mile from the Mormon Temple in Mesa, and there were several hundred Mormons in her high school. Jennifer saw lots of Mormon girls get married young, and she didn't want that. But I was certain about what I wanted. "Please marry me this summer," I insisted. "Come with me to Illinois."

A few days later, in what I have come to love about her decisive, measured style, she looked at me and simply said, "Okay, I'll marry you this summer." I couldn't believe my ears. After I walked her to the dorm and kissed her good night, I sprinted two blocks to the park across the street from my apartment. Dancing through the grass, making pirouettes, I struck the air with my fists and shouted at the top of my voice, "Yes. Yes. Yes." We chose July 8, just two months away, for a summer wedding at Central Christian Church in Mesa, Arizona. The next day, I resigned from my job, effective June

20. After her finals in May, we drove across Kansas and I introduced her to my parents and my hometown. Two days later, I
took Jennifer on to Denver, from where she flew to Phoenix. For
the next month, I finished up my job at the college and we
exchanged love letters. Forty-five years later, I still feel like the
luckiest man alive.

19

CHRISTMAS SUNDAY IN THE
LAND OF NUMB

When Jennifer returned to Phoenix for Christmas break after her first semester, we were not yet engaged, but I did not want to be without her that Christmas. I did not want to be in Colby, either, but even more, I did not want to be alone. So back to Colby I drove to spend Christmas week with my family. Jennifer was on my mind way more than Christmas, as I counted the days until January 1, when I would make a work trip to Phoenix and, of course, see Jennifer. Meanwhile, in early December the college development office had asked me if I would be interested in preaching on Christmas morning in Scott City, 70 miles south of Colby. I said yes. That meant not going to church with my family on Christmas Day, which made Mom unhappy. Adding to her annoyance was that I was back home for a couple of days before telling Mom and Dad I would preach in Scott City on Christmas morning and not go to church with the family. When I told them I would be gone Christmas morning, Mom responded in a disgusted voice, "Oh, are you kidding? Do you have to go to Scott City? We are going to have a Christmas breakfast and all go to church together."

"Mom," I said, "The church doesn't have a minister right now. The college office asked me if I could help them out, and I told them I would."

"You could have told me before you got here. You could have told your boss that you were going to be with your family on Christmas morning, attending church with them. Couldn't that little church have their own people just take turns reading the Christmas story? I feel like you do not want to be with your family." Mom normally couldn't get in touch with her feelings so quickly but she sure did that morning. I didn't mean to disappoint her, but by withholding information, I ended up upsetting her even more.

"Mom, I told them I'd come." She left the room. And I left and went to the *Land of Numb*, sitting down in my old basement bedroom and looking at Grandma Jennings' magazines. On a cloudy, gray, and windy Christmas morning, I headed to Scott City. The first few miles I did not see another vehicle. After pulling into town, I found the church building. The parking lot was empty. I was 45 minutes early. There were no lights on in the building. For 15 minutes I drove around the little town, until going back to the church. Still no cars in the parking lot. I felt stupid for having said I would come and preach on Christmas morning. After I drove around the block a few times, one car appeared in the parking lot. I ran up to the building. The door was unlocked and the lights in the foyer were on. A 70-year-old man in a suit and tie stood near the door, looking like he was waiting for me. "You made it. Are you Mr. Don Follis?"

"Yes sir, I am. Am I at the right place?"

"You sure are. Merry Christmas. I am Sam, the church elder who spoke to the people at the college about having someone come and preach this Christmas Sunday. Thanks for coming. I know you drove down from Colby. That's a long drive by yourself on Christmas morning."

"About 75 miles. Not bad."

"Any other cars on the road?"

"Very few."

"They said you are the public relations officer for the Christian college. Do you like your job?"

"Sure do. Why do you ask?"

"Do you plan to be a full-time preacher any time soon?"

"I'm not really sure about that. Probably some day."

"The reason I ask is that we don't have a minister right now. We might be interested in talking with a young fellow like you." That Christmas morning Sam had gone straight to talking shop. "We had some problems with our minister and we parted company two months ago."

"Sorry to hear that."

"Well, you know, those kinds of things happen. But God is going to take care of us. We figure He's got a purpose in this."

"I am sure he does. Tell me about the service this morning, Sam."

"Well, we won't have many. Maybe 20 people. A few more perhaps. The faithful will be here. They always are." Sam was right. In the next few minutes, 25 people had made their way into the church sanctuary. There were 15 blue-padded pews on each side with an aisle down the middle. At 9 a.m., Sam walked up on stage and sat in a chair behind the pulpit. He had me walk beside him up the aisle from the back of the room. "I'll go on up and sit on the stage. You just sit in the first pew." I followed Sam's instruction.

Sam gave a nod to a woman who walked to the piano and began playing. He stepped to the pulpit and said, "Merry Christmas, Everyone." While we sang *Joy to the World*, Sam walked over to a 6-foot artificial tree and plugged in the lights. After we sang a few other Christmas favorites, Sam made some announcements before looking down at me on the front pew. "We have Mr. Don Follis here this morning to give the Christmas message. This young man drove from Colby this morning—75 miles, just to be with us this Christmas morning. Isn't that something?"

Sam pronounced the "o" of my last name with a long "o," saying it like a young horse – "Foal-lis." When we first met in the church foyer I had corrected him, saying, "It is Follis like the fall of the year: "Fall-us." Still, Sam said, "Let's give Mr. Foal-lis a warm Christmas welcome." The 25 faithful clapped when I stepped up to the pulpit.

"Merry Christmas. I'm Don Follis (Fall-us)." All the people sat in the back three pews—all on the same side. Letting out a big breath, I said, "It's nice to be here on Christmas morning. If you have a Bible, please turn to Luke chapter two." For the next 15 minutes, I shared my Christmas sermon with the 25 people all huddled in the back. When I finished, I returned to the front pew. Sam walked back to the pulpit, made a few closing remarks, and said, "Let's all stand and sing *We Wish You a Merry Christmas*." He then clapped his hands once like they were cymbals and said, "Well folks, let's go home and make merry. God bless you and have a very Merry Christmas." Sam walked over to the artificial tree and unplugged the lights. The faithful filed out. Sam walked up to me, shook my hand and said, "Merry Christmas, Mr. Foal-lis. Thank you for coming."

"Merry Christmas, Sam."

Where are you headed now?"

"Back to Colby."

"Sorry you had to drive so far by yourself this Christmas morning."

"That's okay. I'll be *Just Fine*."

"I guess you'll have a Christmas dinner with your family?"

"That's right, Sam. Planning on it. How about you?"

"Same. This is the day to make merry."

"Indeed it is."

"If you want more information about what kind of minister we're looking for here, give me a call. This is a nice community. Lots of good people." We ended as we had begun—just Sam and me, shaking hands in the lobby. "I better lock her up and get home for my Christmas brunch. My wife is waiting in the car." Sam handed me a check for $50 and said, "Here's a little Christmas gift. Thanks again for coming." When I got in my car, my watch said 9:50. Start to finish the service had taken less than an hour. As I drove north out of Scott City, I found a radio station playing Christmas carols to keep me company. If you had told me on that lonely drive back to Colby that the very next Christmas Jennifer would be my wife—standing with her arm around my waist singing *Joy to the World*—I would have looked at you with utter incredulity.

20

MEETING JIMMY

Jennifer and I did get married and move to Champaign-Urbana. And while I wasn't preaching at a church, I was leading university students in their faith journey and continuing my own. I quickly learned that God's Church was much bigger and more diverse than I had previously experienced. Early on in my campus ministry tenure a friend told me about St. John's Catholic Newman Center and Newman Hall that sat right in the heart of campus. "It's a great place to meet students," he said. "You have to get to know it. You can buy coffee or lunch. You can study and write your Bible studies." The cafeteria was underneath the chapel. Wooden tables and chairs in long rows lined the room. Throughout the day, professors and graduate students mixed in with the residents eating their meals and studying. Off in the corners, priests were surrounded by four or five students. I came to love the place. For many years that cafeteria was my "office." Sometimes I arrived at 8 a.m.; sometimes it was 2 p.m. Whenever I arrived, it smelled like institutional spaghetti.

Way in the back, a wooden table sat directly under an

exhaust fan that drowned out noise from the rest of the cafeteria. That was my spot. I had hundreds of student appointments sitting at a table under that exhaust fan. Students knew where to find me and often came looking for me to buy them a Coke or a cup of coffee, hoping I'd have time to talk. I developed a habit of making notes on napkins. When a meeting ended, I handed the student my napkin notes. Years later a student who returned to campus for a visit reminded me of the napkins and said, "You owe Newman Hall 50 boxes of napkins."

"Way more than that," I said, laughing.

"Man, I wish I had kept all those napkin notes you wrote," he said. "They were full of Scripture references and great insights. I would have written a commentary and called it 'The Napkin Commentary—A Theology Primer.'"

Limping to the drone of the fan was Jimmy, the ubiquitous bus boy. He cleared tables and talked with everyone—maybe talking more than clearing tables. But the talking was part of his job. He knew everybody; he liked everybody; everybody liked him. Jimmy's left leg didn't bend, so when he pushed his bus cart across the black and white floor tiles, he rocked from side to side.

Every time he saw me, he greeted me in his gravelly voice. "How are you, Donny?"

Pointing toward him I responded, "It's my man—Jimmy."

"Got your place cleared for you," he responded, nodding toward the back of the cafeteria.

One day I said, "Jimmy, how long have you been busing tables here at the Newman Hall cafeteria? A hundred years?"

Furrowing his brow and putting his finger along the side of his temple, he said, "Donny, I don't remember. Since about 1960. What year is this?"

"1985, Jimmy."

"Yep, since 1960."

"Twenty-five years then. Wow."

"Twenty-five years?"

"1960 plus 25 equals 1985. Right, Jimmy?"

"That's right, Donny. Whew! I've been here a long time."
(Eventually, James "Jimmy" Shaw—bused tables at Newman
Hall 46 years, finally retiring in 2006. In 2008, he died in
Champaign, at age 72.)

Jimmy wore a white apron looped over his neck and tied
around his waist and a Chicago White Sox cap. "You're
meeting some students today for counseling, aren't you
Donny?"

"Sure am, Jimmy."

"Donny, you know sometimes I pray the *Hail Mary* when I
see you having a serious talk with students."

"You mean the 'Hail Mary full of grace the Lord is with
thee' prayer?"

"Yep, that one. That okay?"

"It's more than okay, Jimmy. But I am curious. Why that
one?"

"Donny, that's the only one I know," he said, laughing
loudly.

"That's perfect, Jimmy. You keep praying it. I'll receive it as
often as you pray it."

When Jimmy moved on, rocking from side to side with his
cart, I prayed for him, too, praying the same prayer he prayed
for me. "Hail Mary, full of grace, the Lord is with thee. Blessed
art thou among women and blessed is the fruit of thy womb,
Jesus. Holy Mary, Mother of God, pray for us sinners—both
Jimmy and me—now and at the hour of our death. Amen."

The next time I saw I him I told him I also prayed the *Hail
Mary* that very day he told me he prayed it over me. "That okay
with you, Jimmy?" Jimmy laughed out loud, just as he had
when he told me the *Hail Mary* was the only prayer he knew.

"That's great, Donny. You pray it for me, and I'll pray it for you."

For years almost every time Jimmy saw me he winked and said, "Remember our prayer, Donny."

"I'm still praying for you, Jimmy."

"I know you are, Donny. You are a man of prayer."

21

THE SIGN OF THE CROSS

Along with Jimmy in the cafeteria, I met Father David Turner, a priest at the Newman Center in the mid-1980s. He loved to gather students around him to discuss theology, politics, or whatever was on their minds. He talked loudly. Father David, a Benedictine priest, was an intellectual with strong opinions about everything and he wasn't afraid to share them. One day when Father David and I drank coffee and chatted, he asked me, "How often do you go up into the chapel to pray, Brother Follis?" He always called me Brother Follis.

"Never."

Laughing, Father David said, "Say it's not so, Brother Follis. My goodness, you need to go up there every week to pray. It's such a great place to think and pray. I see you all the time here meeting students. We want you here. But God wants to meet you in the chapel, too. It's such a beautiful, sacred space. It's here for people just like you."

"Thank you, Father David. I'll go up there sometime."

"Do you have 15 minutes?"

"Sure."

"Great. I am assigning you to go up to the chapel right now —to pray. You can leave your backpack with me." When Father David said that, I froze, thinking back to the summer day in my childhood when my friend Kim and I rode our bikes up to the entryway of St. Frances Cabrini Catholic Church in Hoxie, Kansas. "Dare you to go in," Kim said.

I slowly opened the tall wooden door and tip-toed into the church. Kim tucked himself right in behind me. We tiptoed down the aisle in the dark sanctuary and were near the altar at the front when a nun dressed in her black habit opened a door near the front of the sanctuary. "What are you boys doing?" Without saying a word, we spun around and bolted out of the church and rode to my house as fast our legs would pedal.

Someone who saw us run out of the church building recognized us and told my mom. Later that day she confronted me. "Did you and Kim go inside the Catholic Church today?"

"Yes."

"Don't you ever go into that Catholic Church again or something worse could happen to you."

"Like what?" I asked.

"Believe me, you don't want to know."

When Father David realized my mind had gone somewhere else, he asked me, "Are you okay, Brother Follis?"

"Oh, I'm sorry. My mind wandered. Yeah, I'm okay Father David. I'll go up to the chapel. Tell me what to do." I expected instructions, and I got them.

"Brother Follis, before you enter the chapel, be sure to bless yourself with the holy water from the font just outside the double doors leading into the chapel."

"Bless myself? I'm not Catholic, Father David."

"That doesn't matter in the least, Brother Follis."

"How do I do that?"

"Once you get to the font, dip your fingers—your thumb, index and middle fingers—into the font of holy water. Press your fingers down into the sponge. Then make the sign of the cross, praying, 'In the name of the Father, and the Son, and the Holy Spirit.' Simple as that. Ever done that before?"

"Nope."

"Look at my hand," he said, tracing the sign of the cross on himself with his right hand. "Now let's do it together." A dozen people were scattered at tables nearby. Seeing me looking around, embarrassed, instead of watching him, Father David laughed and said, "Don't be nervous, Brother Follis. Relax. You can't get this wrong. You're in a Catholic student center, for crying out loud." This time as Father David led out, I followed, moving my fingers from my forehead, to the center of my chest and then to my left shoulder and across to my right shoulder.

"You got it," Father David said, smiling. A student next to us was mesmerized by the lesson. Always the teacher, Father David explained. "For the Catholic, dipping fingers in the holy water and making the sign of the cross is a sign of baptism. The holy water is sacramental."

"Sacramental?"

"That's right. Dipping your hand in the water and making the sign of the cross reminds us of the sacrament of baptism." Straightening in his chair, Father David clapped his hands three times and pointed me toward the chapel. "Okay, time's a-wasting. Get yourself up to the chapel. Quickly now, before you lose your gumption."

I walked up from the basement cafeteria to the main floor and stood at the back of the chapel. I saw only two people inside. Taking a big breath, I dipped my three fingers into the sponge in the bottom of the basin of holy water. Raising my right hand, I made the sign of the cross, quietly saying, "In the name of the Father, the Son, and the Holy Spirit." Opening the double glass doors, I walked all the way to the front, finally sitting down on the second wooden pew on the left side. I pulled down the red vinyl kneeler and knelt on the cushioned pad. Directly on the wall in front of me was a 9-foot by 6-foot copy of the Apostles' Creed, the same one from St. Isidore's in Manhattan. So I read:

> "*I believe in God the Father Almighty, creator of heaven and earth; I believe in Jesus Christ His only Son our Lord. He was conceived by the Holy Spirit and born of the Virgin Mary. He suffered under Pontius Pilate, was crucified, died and was buried. He descended to the dead. On the third day he rose again. He ascended into heaven and is seated at the right hand of the Father. He will come again to judge the living and the dead.*
>
> "*I believe in the Holy Spirit, the holy catholic church, the communion of saints, the forgiveness of sins, the resurrection of the body and the life everlasting.*"

For the next 10 minutes I sat quietly, concentrating on my breathing. Finally I left the sanctuary, walking back through the glass doors before once again dipping my fingers into the baptismal font, and making the sign of the cross as I prayed, "In the name of the Father, the Son, and the Holy Spirit." When I walked back to the cafeteria, Father David was reading. My backpack sat on top of the table. "Well," Father David said, "You're smiling, Brother Follis. How did it go?"

"It was good. I followed your instructions."

"Perfect. You are welcome to go into the chapel anytime you like. Please don't be a stranger up there."

"I won't be." And I wasn't. I started going into the chapel two or three times a week. Since I met so many students in the cafeteria, it was easy when I was between appointments to go up into the chapel to read and pray. One day I fell asleep for 30 minutes. That large sanctuary became a place where I felt relaxed and safe. Often I just sat, slowly breathing and looking up at the marble crucifix high above the altar at the front of the sanctuary. A statue of the Madonna stands on one side of the crucifix, while a statue of John, the beloved disciple of Jesus, stands on the other.

One day after noon Mass had cleared out, I got a real surprise. Walking into the foyer, I blessed myself at the baptismal font and went to the pew where I always sat. No more than a minute passed as I looked up at the crucifix. Tears filled my eyes as suddenly I felt as if Jesus were speaking directly to me. "You know you are God-breathed, don't you, Don? My Father and I created you, breathing life into your lungs when you were born in that little rural hospital way out in northwestern Kansas. You are my son, and I am so proud of you. I have never thought anything less." Never had I heard anything like that.

Feeling drawn to the account of Jesus' baptism in Matthew chapter 3, I pulled my Bible out of my backpack and read:

"...At that moment heaven was opened and he—John the Baptist —saw the Spirit of God descending like a dove and alighting on him. And a voice from heaven said, 'This is my son, whom I love; with Him I am well pleased.'" Matthew 3:16-17.

"That's how I feel about you, Don," I felt God say. "You are my son—*my beloved*." Turning my palms upward, I sat quietly, basking in God's presence. Over the years, I returned to that chapel a hundred times, gazing at the crucifix, and thinking about what it meant for God to call me His *beloved*.

Just before Thanksgiving, Father David and I met for coffee in the cafeteria. He reached down to the chair next to him and grabbed a red hard-bound book. The gold-embossed letters on the front cover read *The New Catholic Study Bible ... St. Jerome Edition.*

"Open it, Brother Follis." On the dedication page I read, written in black ink from a fountain pen, "*Presented to Donald D. Follis On Thanksgiving 1985 By David Turner, O.S.B.*" I knew that O.S.B. signifies that Father David is of the Order of Saint Benedict. I have no idea how he knew my given name was Donald or that my middle initial was D.

"This is my gift to you, Brother Follis, as my dear brother in Christ."

"Thank you so much. What a beautiful gift."

"May the peace of Christ fill your heart as you read and meditate on God's Word all the days of your life," he said. When I stood to leave, Father David, a burly man with a bald head, opened his arms, hugged me tightly and said, "I love you, Brother Follis. Happy Thanksgiving."

"I love you, too, Father David." As I walked back across campus, I turned and looked back at St. John's Catholic Chapel. Just as He had that day in the chapel as I gazed upon the crucifix, I felt God speak again. This time, He was saying, "Father David is My *beloved*, too."

PART FOUR
DECIDING TO LEAVE
THE LAND OF NUMB

22

I AM NOT ASHAMED OF YOU

Our kids were both born in Urbana, Illinois. Ian James in 1986, and Madeline Ruth in 1989. When they were young, we drove from Illinois to Colby to see my parents at least once a year. Door-to-door it was 804 miles. Because I wanted to get there in one day, we were on the road by 5:30 a.m. Setting the cruise on 75 mph, we rolled. Around Kansas City we pulled over, ate lunch out of the cooler and let the kids burn off some energy. After lunch we drove the final 400 miles straight across Kansas on Interstate 70.

There never was much of a plan when we got to Colby. Mom showed her loved with food—cinnamon rolls, pies and dad's favorite—pot roast with potatoes, carrots, and onions. Dad had worked his whole life. Working was his hobby. He liked it if I helped him wash his car and pickup. In the evening, he drove us around and showed us any new houses or building projects in the town that he loved. Dad and Mom lived in Colby until Dad's death in May of 2009. He never wanted to live anywhere else.

Our most significant trip out west was in the early 1990s.

Because of my failed early marriage, I never much liked returning to Colby. Unlike Dad, I had little attachment to the place. That trip was during county fair week. One afternoon while Jennifer and the kids went with my folks to see the parade, I stayed back and sat on the porch reading. That night, Jennifer and I got our kids to sleep and took a walk. After walking a mile, we sat down on a bench in the city park.

She spoke first. "You really don't like coming back here, do you?"

"Nope. I like for the kids to see Dad and Mom, but that's about it. "

After a silence, Jennifer said, "I want to say something."

"Go ahead."

"I am really happy to be married to you."

"I am happy to be married to you, too." I knew there was more.

"I am proud to be your wife. I want to say something important. We have two beautiful children. We have a good life. You are a good husband, a good Dad, and a good campus pastor. When I chose you, I knew you had been divorced, and that didn't matter to me. When I said 'I do,' I meant it. I still mean it."

"I like hearing that."

"And here's what I want to say to you: I am not ashamed of you. You don't have to feel ashamed in Colby or anywhere else. You can walk downtown in the daylight. I wish you would."

I always knew that Jennifer accepted me and loved me. But as we walked back to my parents' home, I felt it like never before. The power of the *Land of Numb* lessened that night.

23
NOT JUST FINE

Our daughter Maddie was four when she jumped off the back porch and landed hard on her elbow. We ended up in the emergency room, where she was diagnosed with a slight fracture. She needed a sling, not a cast. However, that diagnosis took all afternoon and evening as we waited for the x-ray, the doctor and the discharge papers. When we got home, we all were exhausted. After finally getting Maddie to sleep, Jennifer and I plopped down on the couch. Jennifer asked me, "How do you feel?"

"*Just Fine,*" I said.

Instantly, the flat of Jennifer's hand smacked the coffee table. Kaboom! "You cannot be fine, mister. Fine is a grade of sandpaper!"

"But I am fine."

"No, you're not. You can be scared. You can be angry. You can be thankful. You can be relieved. But you cannot be fine."

"Okay, I am not *Just Fine.*"

"Great," Jennifer said. "Would you like a do-over?"

"Yes, please."

"All right. How are you feeling?"

"Thankful, relieved and exhausted."

"Me, too," Jennifer said. Bending toward me, she kissed my forehead and said, "Let's go to bed."

It was a decisive moment—though just a baby step—on the journey of leaving the *Land of Numb*. My next lesson came at the jail.

———

I was part of a team that visited inmates at the Champaign County jail once a month. One Sunday, it was my turn to preach. One inmate in particular said a loud "Amen" to almost everything I said. When we broke into groups, he was in mine. A topless woman was tattooed on his right forearm. Putting that arm around my shoulder, he said, "How you been feeling this week, Preacher? You okay?"

"I'm *Just Fine*, Brother."

"*Just Fine*? Now wait a minute, Preacher," he said, giving me a suspicious look. You can't be fine. I'm sure of that."

"Really?"

"Of course, Preacher. Do you know what fine means?"

"I think I'm about to find out."

Every man in the room gave rapt attention to their fellow inmate. "Preacher, you need to get yourself to some AA meetings so you can learn all about being fine. But I'm going to teach right now. Can I get an amen?" All 20 inmates in the room shouted loud amens to the man who suddenly had become the preacher.

"Preacher, F means fouled up." Except he used a more colorful word. It was the first time I had ever heard the F-word used in a church service. "Can I get an amen, brothers?"

"Amen!" the men in orange jumpsuits shouted.

"We're keeping it real here today, aren't we, brothers?"

"That's right. That's right. We're keeping it real."

"I stands for insecure, Preacher."

"Amens" rang out.

"N is for naïve." More amens. "And E means egotistical."

"Amen! Amen!"

"That's what fine means, Preacher. Is that what you are?"

"No, sir," I shouted back. Twenty amens bounced off the walls of the windowless room. One man stood up and shouted, "You ain't fine, Preacher. No sir. You ain't fine."

I ventured, "Could you ask me again how I am feeling?"

Laughing out loud, he said, "How are you feeling, Preacher?"

"I am feeling blessed. Content. Encouraged. Joyful!"

"Whoo-wee!" he bellowed. "There's some emotion there, Preacher. Yes sir! You got some good emotion. Can I get an amen, brothers?"

"Amen!" "Hallelujah" and "Praise Jesus!" filled the room.

"There you go, Preacher," he said. "See what I mean. You ain't *Just Fine*. Nobody ever is fine. You got it?"

"I got it."

———

The more I pressed into being fully present, the more I realized that the words from the inmate were exactly right. No one ever is just fine. There are just two kinds of emotions—painful and positive. Every day people answer each other saying, "I am *Just Fine*," but that is just a greeting, a way of responding to, "Hello, how are you?" I'm not talking about that use of the word. I'm talking about the *Just Fine* that dismisses the situation and stuffs the emotion. The brother at jail is right, and Jennifer is right. Fine is a grade of sand paper. By the mid-1990s, I started to read the Gospels with a new question. What emotion was Jesus feeling? He sure wasn't fine when he told his own mother his time had not yet come before he turned the water into wine. Jesus wept when his friend Lazarus died. That's not being *Just Fine*. And no one would ever say he was fine when he cried out from the cross "My God, My God, why have you forsaken me?" Jesus had painful and positive emotions like all humans, and I was getting closer to being able to feel my own, getting a little less numb.

24
AT LAST!

When I had been in campus ministry 15 years, I wanted to move on to something else. Even my Grandma Follis had asked me, "When are you going to be a real minister?" Believe me, campus ministry makes you a real minister. "Don't worry, Grandma," I said. "I'm already a real minister through and through." What she meant was, when are you going to be the pastor of a congregation, of an actual church. Though I thought I wanted to move from campus ministry to pastor a congregation, one unspoken reason I stayed in campus ministry was that I didn't want to get into it with a church hiring committee about the issue of divorce. I kept that fear tucked down inside of me, but it was there, and I never had dealt with it. So I tried other things.

I thought about starting a church in Denver. But during the winter visit to Colby when I had planned to take Jennifer on over to Denver to talk to the church planters, I chickened out. "When are we visiting Denver?" she asked. I mumbled that we weren't going after all. She didn't push. She told me later that she hadn't wanted to do that anyway but had been willing to investigate it with me. So, no Denver. I didn't have to hear a church tell me "no" if I told myself "no" first.

In the early 1990s my thoughts of pastoring a church got diverted when a job announcement in *Christianity Today* magazine for an associate editor caught my eye. I had earned a master's degree in journalism at the University of Illinois, taking classes part time. I had written articles for smaller magazines. CT actually showed interest, getting my hopes up when they asked me to write a short piece and edit a longer one. When they printed my 750-word story, it was so heavily edited I barely recognized it. I did not get a job offer, which helped me realize that was not what I wanted to do anyway. What I wanted to do next was to pastor a church. While continuing to lead a ministry to international students on campus, I pushed on to finding a church to pastor. My applications garnered me trips to Fort Collins, Colorado; Prescott, Arizona; Davis, California; St. Paul, Minnesota; and Wichita, Kansas. Every trip, I told the hiring committees that I was interested in being their next pastor. I put my best foot forward—asking hard questions, carefully listening, and drawing on my campus ministry experience. With one exception, the interviews went well. Some wanted to move ahead with the process. They were positive. The very thing I said I wanted to do—move out of campus ministry and step into leading a church—had presented itself.

Turns out I was not as emotionally healthy as I thought. When the offers came to relocate, and several came, each time I declined a follow-up interview, saying I had decided to stay put. That disappointed and confused the hiring committee. It baffled Jennifer, too. A couple of times I didn't even tell her I had been invited back for a second interview. I only told her I didn't think that church was for me. I stayed firmly entrenched in the *Land of Numb*. While I thought I was keeping myself safe from disappointment and rejection, I actually was trapped, frozen and unable to make healthy, honest decisions. When I turned churches down, it usually led to my putting on my kick-me sign and punishing myself—berating myself with bad names. None of the name calling was true, but it was utterly exhausting. It was what my fear of making a clear, firm decision did to me. I could really let myself have it. Ironically, pastors I befriended often applauded me for helping them make important decisions in their lives. You'd think I could make my own.

———

I know now that I cannot be fully present if I insist on being *Just Fine*. When you're *Just Fine*, you shut off the pathway to feeling both painful and positive emotions. As I look back on my life, it was not that there was a lack of love in my family, and certainly not a lack of hard work. Dad and Mom were hard-working Christian people, both of them loving, friendly and good-hearted. But they didn't do emotions well, at least not that I heard. They were deeply rooted in the *Land of Numb* where you never have to make clear decisions, especially decisive ones that scare you and require taking a risk that might be costly emotionally. Not making a clear decision allows you to evade one of Jesus' most important instructions: "Let your yes be yes, and your no, no." (Matthew 5:37). The Apostle Paul said it like this: "Speak the truth in love." He didn't say, "Let me think about it for several years so I can know with certainty that whatever I choose, everyone will like me."

I credit one family vacation in particular that taught me

how to evade decisions. I was in junior high. The plan was for us to go for a week to stay in lakeside cabins provided by Dad's company. As we gathered up our gear, Dad announced at the last minute that he had a lot of work to do at the office and would have to arrive a couple of days late and drive up by himself. Dad and Mom fought over it, an argument that left Mom in tears. From day one Dad had committed to go with us. We all thought he was all in for the entire vacation, but he wasn't. We didn't know that until the last minute. When Mom challenged him, he was aggressive and said, "You are just going to have to understand there are times I have more work to do than I expected." His indecisiveness and lack of clarity made us all feel terrible.

Without him on that Sunday afternoon, we packed the car and Mom drove us to the lake. Dad showed up Tuesday evening, saying that he had gotten everything done and acting as though nothing uncomfortable had ever happened. If he had said from the beginning that he couldn't go for the entire week, we would not have been so confused and disappointed. But it didn't matter in the end because we all said we were *Just Fine.*

Even though work can be an excuse for not making decisions, work still can be good and meaningful. And I did learn how to work. I still laugh about Dad's "favorite Bible verse"—*Work Harder!* That part I got. And in fact, though I may not have been leading a church, I was leading a campus ministry, where I constantly read, planned, studied, and wrote. I bought and read hundreds of books. One of the authors whose books I read more than once was Eugene Peterson, the author of *The Message*, Peterson's paraphrase of the Bible. My introduction to

Peterson's books came just after our daughter Maddie was born in 1989. As a baby gift, a campus ministry friend brought me a copy of *A Long Obedience in the Same Direction*. Handing me the book, he said, "Congratulations on the birth of your daughter. While she's sleeping, here's a book for you to read and ponder."

Peterson's book captured my imagination as he described the Songs of Ascent (Psalms 120-134) and how pilgrims sang these songs on their way to worship in Jerusalem. He argues that a life of discipleship is about showing up each day, developing healthy spiritual rhythms, and starting our day full of gratitude and wonder.

I moved on to Peterson's pastoral trilogy, which helped me refine my inner life. In the first of the three, *Five Smooth Stones for Pastoral Work*, Peterson shows how five Old Testament books—Esther, Song of Solomon, Ecclesiastes, Ruth, and Lamentations—give a foundation for pastoral work. *Working the Angles* encouraged me to keep embracing what I had told students for years about the inner life—read widely; make room for doubt; and accept that life is full of mystery. While reading *Working the Angles* I started writing in a journal—now a 30-year practice. In *Under the Unpredictable Plant: An Exploration in Vocational Holiness*, Peterson argues that *being* is more important than *doing*. In book three, Peterson calls pastors out for their preoccupation with image, measurable success, community standing, and for always saying they are so busy.

Whenever I need to remember the essence of my faith, I read Romans 8, especially in Peterson's paraphrase. I put *The Message* alongside my New International Version every day, now on the BibleGateway website. In the summer of 1999, *Christianity Today* magazine announced that Peterson would speak at a pastor's conference at *Kanuga Conference, Retreat and Camp Center*, a ministry of the Episcopal Church in North

Carolina. I jumped at the chance to meet him and signed up to go. When I arrived, I thought I was off to a good start when the room assigned to me was the same room used by writer Madeleine L'Engle not long before. Peterson spoke the first morning, reading from his manuscript. Although his content was rich, his delivery was flat and his voice raspy. The guy sitting beside me said, "You have to sit up on the edge of your chair and really pay attention with Peterson." Following the morning session, I ate lunch quickly and walked out to a porch that overlooked Lake Kanuga at the base of the mountains.

Near me was a balding, lean man. It was Peterson. "How are you?" he asked. "I don't believe we've met. I'm Eugene Peterson."

"Nice to meet you, Mr. Peterson. I'm Don Follis."

"Just call me Gene. What brings you here this week, Don?"

"You did."

"Well, thank you. I am pleased to meet you. I think I came here to talk with you," he said, smiling. Looking out at the Blue Ridge Mountains beyond Lake Kanuga, Peterson said, "You ever hiked in these mountains?"

"Nope. This is my first time to come to Kanuga."

"Me, too."

"It's a lovely view."

"Do you have any plans right now?"

"No. I was going back to my cabin to read."

"What do you say we take a hike? If you're up to it."

After getting a trail map from the camp office, we headed off on a route that took us around Lake Kanuga and into the mountains. For the next 90 minutes, we talked about our families, our ministries, where we lived, and, of course, writing. Usually I am the guy who asks the questions, but for the first 30 minutes Peterson did the asking. When I answered, Peterson urged me on, saying, "Tell me more about that."

When we stopped to sit on a bench and catch our breath, I brought up that I had begun writing a Sunday religion column for the Champaign-Urbana, Illinois, *News-Gazette*.

"Have any ideas for me?" I asked him.

"Wow," he said. "Congratulations. My idea is this—keep writing it. What an opportunity to influence your city."

"I think so."

"Do you like the immediate feedback you get from people?"

"Yes, I do."

"Sounds like writing a religion column fits you well. The books I write aren't published for a year or more after I submit the manuscript. By then I've moved on to the next project."

After we made our way back to the dining hall, Peterson said, "Thanks for hiking with me. I really enjoyed it. I hope this religion column goes on for a long time. That deadline will keep you focused." When I returned home, I threw myself into writing the column, often writing about one of the central themes I saw in Peterson's books: "Being is more important than doing." I hope my readers consider that who they are is way more important than what they do. Not long ago I received a hand-written note from a retired teacher. "I've been reading your column for years," she wrote. "I've cut out at least a hundred of them and put them in a shoe box. My children live all across the United States. I've copied and sent many of your columns to them. And by the way, I'm not *Just Fine*. I'm glad you aren't either."

———

When I turned down the churches that were ready to hire me, it was not because I was afraid of hard work. It was because I was afraid of being rejected. Now I know that. Looking back, I see how ridiculous that was. If I didn't go back for a second interview, I didn't have to find out if they would pick me or not. The *Land of Numb* carefully shielded me from feeling the full weight of either painful or positive emotions. If I were going to be totally present, I had to allow myself to feel them all.

The church that was the best fit for me was in Minneapolis/St. Paul, next to the University of Minnesota. It was full of broad-minded people who had a heart for justice, simplicity, and caring for the poor. They were glad I had campus ministry experience on a Big Ten campus, especially with international students. The head of the search committee told me, "I feel like you'd be perfect for us, and I really hope you and your family will come." I said I'd let them know. I put off the decision. I asked about schools. The weather. I may as well have been asking if they had air to breathe. I delayed with more questions. I was ridiculous. After weeks of being patient, the search committee finally made the decision for me and moved on without me. Once again, the *Land of Numb* allowed me to avoid making a solid decision to say yes or no. When that happened, my passive-aggressive side complained that I hadn't been given enough time to make the decision, which was utterly preposterous. No place is ever perfect. But by declining the chance to emotionally embrace the opportunity before me, I missed the opportunity to grow spiritually. Or gain respect from my family. Jennifer hated the *Land of Numb*, but what could she do? She was patient with me. But the 1990s tried her patience.

———

In coaching pastors now, I often ask them, "What do you think is underneath the surface of what you are feeling?" That's what I had to figure out for myself. I came to realize that my struggle was like a scene in the *The Great Divorce* by C.S. Lewis, where people living in hell—a very grey town in the book—are given the chance to take a bus ride to heaven. The book is Lewis' study of the difference between living in heaven and living in hell. In hell people become increasingly isolated from each other until they lose all communication. Before the great distances develop, there is a bus stop where people can go to heaven on a tour bus to see if they want to move there. Most bus riders return to hell. My favorite naysayer is a bishop, whose self-importance holds him back. He has to return to hell because he is scheduled to give a lecture.

When people arrive in heaven, they are met by spirits who invite them to stay and work on the unique character flaws that drove them to hell in the first place. Lewis says the gates of hell are locked from the inside. Those in hell choose to be there. In the end, he says there are only two kinds of people: "Those who say to God, 'Thy will be done,' and those to whom God says in the end, 'Thy will be done.'"

One bus rider has an engorged lizard on his shoulder who tries to convince him that life in heaven would be miserable. In his case, the lizard is the embodiment of lust. An angel tells the man that the lizard must be killed. "May I kill it?" the angel asks, unwilling to act against the man's will. Reluctantly, the man finally agrees. But the man is convinced that when the lizard dies, he, too, will die.

When the angel breaks the lizard's back, the man shrieks in agony, believing he surely is dying. Both the lizard and the man look dead. But then the fellow rises into a magnificent man, and the lizard grows into a marvelous stallion. They go off into heaven, while the rest of the people on the bus return to hell and become ever more alienated from each other.

The lizard on my shoulder said, "You are a gifted pastor, Don—a good preacher, a fine student, well read, an engaging conversationalist, a good counselor—but you had better not make a decision to take the reins in one of these churches, becoming its pastor. We both know what could happen. You once got rejected by the church. That might happen again, especially if you leave campus ministry. You are intrigued about going off to be a lead pastor. But you never know. What if you fail again? It's not worth the risk. You are divorced and remarried, remember."

My unconscious answer to my lizard was, "You're right. It is not worth the risk." The memories held me back. When an opportunity arose to say "yes," and a decision was imminent, fear grabbed me around the neck and threw me right back into the *Land of Numb*.

In those years, Paul's words in Romans 7 seemed to describe me.

For I have the desire to do what is good, but I cannot carry it out. For I do not do the good I want to do, but the evil I do not want to do—this I keep on doing. ... For in my inner being I delight in God's law, but I see another law at work in me, waging war against the law of my mind and making me a prisoner of the law of sin at work within me. What a wretched man I am! Who will rescue me from this body that is subject to death? Romans 7:18-25.

Finally this struggle came to a head. After backing away with a *No thanks* to several churches, I decided to take a job in town with InterVarsity Christian Fellowship, as the liaison for their five-day triennial student mission conference called URBANA. It was named for the town where I lived, and I wouldn't have to move. The conference was held on the University of Illinois campus. The job open was to lead a team who would spend 18 months organizing the local logistics for the conference to make room for 17,000 students and 200 mission agencies.

Though it was a big job—an administrative monster that did not play to my strength—there was an even bigger problem than the scope of the work. I accepted the job without telling Jennifer. She knew of the opportunity and that I had spoken with the conference officials about it. But that's all she knew. She expected I would talk it over with her. While she didn't know all about how I ducked out of some of the church interviews, I did keep telling her we were going to move to pastor a church. That's what she was expecting, and she kept herself flexible and ready to move.

By taking the InterVarsity job, I did the opposite of moving on. When I told Jennifer, she was aghast—mad and completely puzzled. For her, that was a tipping point. She kept thinking we were going to move. She was willing to move. She thought I would be a good fit for several of these places. How in the world could I now have taken this job in town without consulting her? Jennifer was about to lose respect for me, and I knew it. After I told her what I did, she took action—no longer willing to wait for my career decisions, my indecisiveness, or my waiting to hear a clear call from God. She turned her part-time job into full-time teaching and advising journalism students at the University of Illinois. She would emphasize her own career. She would have a retirement plan. She would decide.

Following the InterVarsity job, I did accept a pastoral position, joining the team at the Vineyard Church in Urbana. While Jennifer had reservations about some Vineyard theological positions, she saw that the church allowed remarried people to be pastors and we wouldn't have to move. We no longer talked about my leaving and gallivanting off somewhere to take a lead ministry.

But way more significant, something was about to change in my heart that would move the ball down the field. In the final weeks of the *InterVarsity* job, I read Peter Scazzero's book called *The Emotionally Healthy Church—A Strategy for Discipleship that Actually Changes Lives* (Zondervan, 2003). I read it cover to cover twice in two days. Finally I was ready to be more than *Just Fine*. Never had I had such a strong desire to get out of the *Land of Numb*. It was Scazzero's book that turned up the heat and helped my numbness thaw.

Scazzero connected emotional and spiritual health in a way I was ready to hear. I knew I couldn't heal until I attended to what was happening deep within me, until I faced the *Land of Numb* head on. The book drills home six strategies, ideas that I was ready to embrace in ways I never had before.

Looking beneath the surface.

Breaking the power of the past.

Living in brokenness and vulnerability.

Accepting limitations.

Embracing grief and loss.

Making incarnation the model for loving well.

I was ready. The lizard on my shoulder was about to die. Along with *The Emotionally Healthy Church*, I reread Daniel Goleman's *Emotional Intelligence—Why it Can Matter more than IQ* (Bantam Books, New York, 1995). Goleman argues that our emotional intelligence is our ability to identify, understand, and handle emotions in ourselves and in others. When I read Goleman's book a second time—putting it alongside Scazzero's book—I marked up nearly every page.

But it was Scazzero's book that helped me pull back the layers. I knew that if I couldn't embrace what Scazzero said, I might be destined to spend the rest of my ministry and even my marriage, operating out of the *Land of Numb*. That really scared me. It was the last thing I wanted. My way was not working. The day after I finished *The Emotionally Healthy Church* for the second time, I called the New Life Fellowship Church in Queens, New York, where Scazzero was the pastor. When the receptionist answered, I told her, "I think the book saved my life. I want to bring Peter to Champaign-Urbana, Illinois, where I live. He has a powerful message that pastors and leaders in my city need to hear. I need to hear the message every day for the rest of my life." She laughed, saying she was happy the book touched me so deeply. After taking my phone number, she said that Scazzero was a busy man and the chance of him coming to east-central Illinois in the next year was remote. If I didn't hear back from him for a couple of weeks or more likely even a month or six weeks, I should not be surprised. "Try calling back in six weeks if you don't hear anything." But the very next afternoon, Peter Scazzero called me. "Hello, this is Pete Scazzero. Is this Don Follis?"

"Hello, Pete. Yes, this is Don. This week I've read your book cover to cover twice. It made a huge impact. I'd like to invite you to come to Champaign-Urbana, Illinois, where I live. I believe I can gather 100 pastors and leaders who need to hear your message about how our emotional and spiritual health are so closely linked. I need it more than anyone."

"That sounds great," Scazzero said. "Let me look at my calendar." We agreed on a date four months away. Given what the secretary at the church had told me, I was thrilled. When I told Scazzero I would make hotel arrangements for both him and his assistant, he responded in his quick-talking New York City, Italian voice.

"No. No. No, Donny. It would be much better for us if we could stay with you, if you and your wife have room, that is, and if we wouldn't be too much of a burden. Then we could have some sweet fellowship and it could save you some money."

And in fact, Scazzero and his assistant stayed in our home. It was great. They were humble, transparent, and fun. The next day 125 pastors and leaders gathered as Scazzero explored what he repeatedly called "the indisputable connection between emotional and spiritual health." He was remarkably candid. He talked about starting a church in Queens, only to have his wife and daughters quit. Yes, they later returned. He confessed to explosions of anger. He talked about missing dinner with his family "plenty of times" because he was too "busy" with his church work. The crowd was totally engaged. While I sat there, my heart burned. I knew, as never before, this was the start of a new day, a new season, a new way of life. I wanted it. I asked the Lord, "Please help me get out of the *Land of Numb.*" I look back on that time with Scazzero with deep gratitude.

Before Scazzero caught his plane back to New York City, I asked if he and his wife would come back to lead a marriage retreat. A year later, Pete and Geri flew out to Illinois and led 70 couples in a two-day event that centered on connecting emotional and spiritual health in a marriage. For two days they drilled home their central message: *Our emotional health and our spiritual health are closely connected. You cannot have a spiritually healthy marriage if your marriage is emotionally unhealthy.*

Sometimes you can change quickly. The Scazzero book and his two trips to Champaign-Urbana were central in helping me move out of the *Land of Numb.* It was more like sprinting like a scared jackrabbit. I saw what I had to do. Thank God for the eyes to see it. In some ways it was a perfect storm. Because I was so frustrated at continually retreating to the *Land of Numb,* I was ready to take action, to let my yes be yes and my no be no. I was ready not to worry about whether everyone liked me or not. I wanted to be able to make decisions without the assurance ahead of time that everything was going to work out perfectly. Like it always had before, right? Of course it hadn't! Jennifer was more ready than I was for me to change. When I pressed in to be more emotionally and spiritually healthy, so did she.

25

JESUS SHOWS EMOTIONS

After hearing how Peter and Geri Scazzero connected their emotional and spiritual lives, I started seeing emotions everywhere. No one seemed *Just Fine* any more. Not even Jesus. I started seeing things in the Gospels I hadn't seen before. I discovered that Jesus expressed all kinds of emotions. Two stories in Luke 7 repeatedly caught my attention. The first, in verses 7-11, records Jesus encountering a funeral procession as he and his entourage walk from Capernaum to Nain. A widow is about to bury her only son. Jesus' heart goes out to the mother, and he immediately springs into action. Stepping into the crowd, Jesus touches the open casket on which the young man lies, telling the young man to get up. The man sits straight up and begins to talk. Jesus gives him back to his mother. Everyone is utterly overwhelmed and news about Jesus spreads throughout the entire region. I try to put myself into the story and imagine the array of painful and positive emotions—compassion, decisiveness, fear, joy and amazement.

The other story is in Luke 7:36-50. Over and over, I read it, trying to imagine all the emotions in play.

36 When one of the Pharisees invited Jesus to have dinner with him, he went to the Pharisee's house and reclined at the table. 37 A woman in that town who lived a sinful life learned that Jesus was eating at the Pharisee's house, so she came there with an alabaster jar of perfume. 38 As she stood behind him at his feet weeping, she began to wet his feet with her tears. Then she wiped them with her hair, kissed them and poured perfume on them.

39 When the Pharisee who had invited him saw this, he said to himself, "If this man were a prophet, he would know who is touching him and what kind of woman she is—that she is a sinner."

Given how poorly Jesus often was treated by the Pharisees, I am surprised Simon invited him to this kind of dinner party. I wonder if Jesus felt suspicious. From the time Jesus arrives, the host essentially avoids him, not even giving him the greeting that was customary in first-century Palestine. Add to this the entry of a woman with a bad reputation who goes straight for Jesus. I try to imagine some of the emotions being felt. Perhaps the woman felt desperate. Simon the host felt critical. The dinner guests were dismissive, or eager for a fight. Jesus felt judged, or challenged, or ready for the teachable moment.

In full view of everyone, this woman falls at Jesus' feet, weeping uncontrollably. If this woman had come for me, I wonder what I might have felt. What if I were at a party with the muckety-mucks of my town and such a woman pulled up next to me. Would I retreat to the *Land of Numb* and freeze there? I'd be nervous for sure. Maybe Jesus felt nervous.

I'm not a fighter, but some people might have fought—either to push the woman away or to yell at Simon for being so rude. That's not what Jesus did. He could have jumped up and left the party, not allowing himself to be the center of attention for whatever motives his host or the woman might have. Jesus did not flee. As we read on, we see that Jesus stayed still, but he was not frozen and he was definitely not in the *Land of Numb.*

Jesus chose to be present. He stayed at the party—physically, emotionally, and spiritually. Verses 40-42 show us a man comfortable in his own skin. He calmly tells a story. Turning to Simon, Jesus said, "Simon, I have something to say." Simon gave him the floor and Jesus proceeded to tell the parable of two debtors who were forgiven—one for a small debt, the other for a huge debt. Then looking at the woman but speaking to the host of the party, Jesus asked, "Which of these two was most grateful?"

I like how Eugene Peterson's *The Message* renders what happened next in verses 43-50.

> [43-47] Simon answered, "I suppose the one who was forgiven the most."
>
> "That's right," said Jesus. Then turning to the woman, but speaking to Simon, he said, "Do you see this woman? I came to your home; you provided no water for my feet, but she rained tears on my feet and dried them with her hair. You gave me no greeting, but from the time I arrived she hasn't quit kissing my feet. You provided nothing for freshening up, but she has soothed my feet with perfume. Impressive, isn't it? She was forgiven many, many sins, and so she is very, very grateful. If the forgiveness is minimal, the gratitude is minimal."
>
> [43-47 48] Then he spoke to her: "I forgive your sins."
>
> [49] That set the dinner guests talking behind his back: "Who does he think he is, forgiving sins!"
>
> [50] He ignored them and said to the woman, "Your faith has saved you. Go in peace."

Jesus' emotional intelligence is in full view as he makes the comparison between the morally respectable Pharisee and the morally bankrupt woman. Her actions could not have been more self-humbling. And Jesus could not have been more emotionally present. Displaying self-assurance and courage, Jesus stood with the woman, even forgiving her sins. Jesus didn't care about his reputation or whether anyone in the room liked him. He was fully present, and that meant standing with the woman come what may. And boy did the men at the party come at Jesus. They were livid when he stood up for the woman, forgiving her sins. Luke tells us exactly what the host thought of the ordeal. "If this man were a prophet, he would know who is touching him and what kind of woman she is—that she is a sinner." But from what Jesus said, Simon is the one who should be ashamed. Jesus defended the woman against the contempt of powerful men.

I was finally realizing that Jesus wasn't only the meek and mild figure so often presented in paintings. He was not merely a man staring off into space while holding a little white lamb. Jesus' courage especially impresses me because I am a guy who likes to be liked. Like a golden retriever, I always want everyone to be my friend. Not Jesus. And there's the rub. I can't have it both ways. I can't help others the way I want to if I'm also expecting to be liked by everyone. As Jennifer once put it, "If being liked is your highest value, especially when you have a chance to speak truth to power, you have the wrong value." There was a new normal forming for me, and being *Just Fine* was not it. Jesus treated the woman the way he wanted to be treated. I decided to be more like Jesus. I decided to be more present. I was farther away from the *Land of Numb* than I used to be and was grateful to God for my progress. Staying present was essential, as my deepest hurt was yet to come.

PART FIVE
GRIEF

26

WRESTLING

Our son Ian died at age 21 of an accidental drug overdose on November 12, 2007. It was the saddest day of my life. I still miss him every day, but life moves on, and so have I—aging, changing, realizing in reluctant sadness that he is no longer with us. He is caught forever like a snapshot.

Ian was a great son—our first child and our only son. He was kind, mannerly, funny, empathetic, quick witted, artistic. Oh, the what-might-have-beens. He could make his sister laugh out loud. Maddie grieved the loss of her brother, just as Jennifer and I grieved the loss of our son. When I think about Ian, my mind floods with memories: watching him on the swim team and the soccer field, climbing on the pyramids in Egypt, and hiking up Cascade Canyon in Grand Teton National Park. His college art teacher told me, "No one could draw like Ian." Ian often handed me cartoon drawings that made me laugh. We have hard memories, too. He started using drugs as a young teen and became addicted. For him, the switch got turned on quickly, something we never understood. By 21, he was trying to get clean; he had entered rehab programs; he wanted sobriety; but he lost his battle.

The weekend before he died, the University of Illinois played the Ohio State Buckeyes in a much-anticipated Big Ten football game in Columbus. That evening Ian came over to our house to eat and watch the showdown. Illinois' record was 8 and 3, but that night they beat the number one ranked Buckeyes and qualified to play in the Rose Bowl in Pasadena. Ian was an art student at Parkland College in Champaign, living in an apartment and working as a server in a restaurant. His sister was a freshman at the University of Illinois in town, living on campus at Stratford House, a co-op for Christian women. When we finished eating, Ian threw himself down on our carpet right next to me. With our heads propped up on big blue pillows, we were shoulder to shoulder. Late in the first half, Ian started playfully teasing me, pushing his shoulder into mine. And then, with no warning, he jumped up and plopped on top of me, yelling, "Hi-Yah! Let's see you take me, big boy."

"Get off me, Ian. I can't see the game."

"Oh, come one. Let's see what you have." As Ian trash talked—insisting I was a total weakling—I jumped up to tackle him but he jumped away, laughing. Looking toward the living room, he pointed and said, "Oh no, Mom's coming." She wasn't, of course, but when I looked he went for the takedown, getting me flat on my back and said, "Never go for the fake." With all his weight on me I began whining, "You're hurting your dad." After I cried uncle, Ian stood up, thrust both fists over his head, and declared victory.

"I didn't think you could handle me, dude."

"You're the champ, pal," I said, giving him a high five. At the time, he was in outpatient rehab treatment for those who struggled with substance abuse. That evening, I thought he was doing really well and I breathed a sigh of relief. I knew the wrestling match was his way to stay connected and to show love. His love never was in question. The next day he came over and ate Sunday lunch with us before he went back to his apartment. Later that afternoon I took a bike ride and headed toward the basement apartment where Ian lived near campus. When I arrived, he was on the driveway talking on his cell phone. He saw me and gave me a hand signal that said, "Just a minute. Let me finish this call." After he hung up, we talked about five minutes, as he told me about his upcoming work as a server and about a big art project due that Friday. "Big week," he said.

"Yep. You have a lot to do. I love you. Have a good week, buddy. Hang in there."

"Don't worry. I will. Love you, too, Dad." After peddling half a block, I pulled to the curb and straddled the bike with both feet on the street. Turning around, I saw Ian already was on another call. When he saw me looking back, he pointed at me and waved. Waving back, I watched him a few seconds before turning and heading for home. It was the last time I saw him alive.

27
THE DOORBELL KEPT RINGING

At 1:30 a.m. Tuesday morning on November 13, Jennifer and I jerked awake. "Someone is ringing our doorbell." I hurried to the door and peered through the glass. Two men—one wearing a coroner's jacket and the other a law enforcement uniform—stood shoulder to shoulder, staring at our tomato-red front door. Adrenaline shot through me as I opened the door and stepped barefooted onto the cold front porch. Face to face with the night visitors, I asked, "What happened?" Because I was helping oversee pastoral care, I thought something might have happened to someone in the church. Mostly I was just confused.

The coroner spoke first, asking if I knew Ian Follis. "Of course. He is my son. What's going on?" That response was stronger than my first one. By then, Jennifer was beside me in her robe. The policeman spoke next in a plaintive voice, hesitating before raising his left arm from his side. Opening his hand he showed us Ian's driver's license. "Do you know him?"

"That's my son's driver's license. What is going on?"

"We found your son's body late this evening in his apartment," the officer said. "I'm sorry."

"What? Found him?"

"Sir, he passed," said the coroner. "We found his body. He passed. I'm sorry."

I stepped back until I was pinned to the door, suddenly feeling that I could not breathe. We all moved inside where the men told us the few details they knew. When Ian didn't show up for work, a co-worker called him several times, leaving messages on his phone. Ian never missed a shift, so they finally called the police to do a wellness check. Earlier that night Ian's body had been taken to the morgue. More details would be available the next day, the men said. "I am sorry for your loss," they said in near unison. A few minutes after the men left, I called my pastor and friend Ben Hoerr. He picked up his phone on the first ring. "Hello, this is Ben." "Ben, this is Don Follis. I'm sorry to wake you up, but a policeman and coroner were just here, telling us that Ian died. They found his body."

"I'll be right over."

Next, Jennifer called our friends Mike and Gwynne McQueen. Gwynne answered and Jennifer told her we needed Mike to come over. "It's about Ian." Ben and Mike sat with Jennifer and me for a while—mostly in silence. At 3 a.m., we sent Ben home. Mike slept on our living room couch. Back in bed, Jennifer and I held each other, staring wide awake at the dark ceiling. Already a blanket of death had descended over our house. I was having difficulty breathing. With every breath, I inhaled more sorrow. At 5 a.m. I got up, made coffee and sent Mike home. I called my older sister in Kansas, waking her up. "Darylee, it's Don. Ian died last night. They found his body. The coroner and a police officer rang the doorbell at 1:30."

"Oh no."

"Please call Dad and Mom and the other siblings."

"I am so sorry."

"Yeah, me too. I don't have any more information. I'll be in touch."

We called Maddie at Stratford House. "Mom and I need to come over right away and talk with you." When we arrived Maddie came out on the porch. "We have bad news," I said. "Ian died." Her wail pierced the morning sky. After we wept and held each other, Maddie said she wanted to get ready and just go on to her classes. "I'll come over after class." Jennifer and I got in our car and drove home in silence. We had more calls to make. I dreaded the days ahead.

———

Word of Ian's death spread fast. We had been in our small city for 30 years. We lived just a mile east from the hospital where the kids were born. Lots of people knew our family. Ian and Maddie both had worked as lifeguards at the public pool and played sports growing up. I wrote the Sunday religion column for the local paper. Jennifer taught at the University of Illinois. Family members and friends began coming from far and wide. Neighbors stopped by the house. At one point I counted 10 cars parked along the curb. Pastors Ben Hoerr and Mike McQueen stayed close by. People brought food. Flowers were delivered to our home. A friend assigned herself the job of answering the phone and taking messages. We didn't know what we needed. At one point when our living room was full of people, I walked into my bedroom, locked the door, pressed my forehead against the wall, and wept.

The first sentence of his obituary was the hardest to write: *Ian James Follis, 21, of Urbana died Monday, November 12, 2007, in Urbana.* The second was no easier: *Ian is survived by his parents, Don and Jennifer Follis, and his sister, Maddie Follis, also of*

Urbana. During the visitation at the Vineyard Church, we greeted people for hours as hundreds of people waited in a long line to offer condolences. After the funeral, one by one people returned home. We said good-bye to my parents, Jennifer's mom, and our other relatives. Friends went back to work. An old friend who had flown in from California, flew back home. Maddie went back to campus. A neighbor placed a frozen meatloaf on our doorstep. Jennifer and I cleaned out Ian's apartment, moving robotically, saying nothing. When Jennifer and I sat down to eat on the first night we were alone, she looked at me, waiting for me to pray. After a few seconds I said, "I don't have anything to say."

"Let's just eat," she said. Moving food around our plates, we said nothing. Finally I looked at Jennifer and said, "What do we do now?" She just shrugged her shoulders.

28

NO SORROW LIKE THIS
SORROW

We didn't have a public viewing of Ian's body. He was cremated and we took his ashes in an urn to the church for the services. I didn't want anyone to go to the funeral home to view Ian's body except Jennifer, Maddie, and me. But my dad, Jennifer's mom, and Ian's friend Dan wanted to say their good-byes, and that's understandable. We drove in silence to the funeral home. Looking through my rearview mirror, I saw my Dad's face, looking vacant and despondent. There was nothing *Just Fine* about him that day. At 79, he looked sad and old. The cancer he had contracted was in remission and he was still working full time. But now his grandson had died. That day he looked worn out. Weeks after the funeral, Mom told me as she and Dad drove from Kansas to Illinois and back, Dad kept repeating, "It should have been me who died, not Ian."

The funeral home director took us into a room where six blue upholstered chairs sat against the wall. In the middle of the room Ian's body lay on a metal gurney with black wheels. A white sheet covered his entire body except for his neck and head. Jennifer's mom, Lucy, was the first to walk up and stand quietly next to Ian's body. When she had paid her respects, she returned and sat in one of the blue chairs. Dad was next, and then Ian's friend Dan, who sobbed. Jennifer, Maddie, and I stepped toward the gurney. Maddie stood between Jennifer and me. Moving close to Ian's body, none of us said anything. Finally, Jennifer and I rubbed our hands through his brown hair and over the stubble on his face. I wanted to remember how he looked. Jennifer asked the funeral director to uncover his hands and feet. She wanted to touch him, to be sure it was him. She had massaged those feet just days before.

———

Ian had a tattoo on the inside of his left wrist: *Isa 40:31*. That stands for the Bible verse in the book of Isaiah that reads *But those who wait upon the Lord will renew their strength. They shall mount up with wings as eagles, they shall run and not be weary, they shall walk and not faint.* On New Year's Day 2007, Ian had a powerful epiphany at the grave of Jeff Butler. Jeff was shot and killed at age 27 while flying relief workers as a bush pilot in Kenya. He was buried just east of our house at Mount Olive Cemetery. Isaiah 40:31 is etched on his headstone. Jeff was a family friend, the son of Ron and Carolyn Butler, long-time missionaries in the Democratic Republic of Congo. Our families were close. The Butlers were living in Urbana on furlough the year Jeff died, so they had his body buried there. When Ian visited Jeff's grave that cold January day, he felt God spoke to him, saying, "Ian, if things don't change, you are going to have a short life." Shaken, Ian left the cemetery, drove straight to our home and told us about the encounter. A few days later he walked into the house, stuck out his left arm, and rotated it so we could see his tattoo—*Isa 40:31*.

———

I felt deeply angry and offended by the sheer awfulness of death—offended on behalf of Jennifer who for 21 years loved Ian with all her heart, offended on behalf of Maddie, who lost her brother and only sibling, and offended for myself. I lost my only son, a boy I continue to be proud of. The Bible portrays death as a terrible enemy, and standing next to Ian's body, I felt profoundly offended at death. I said, "Son, you were created to live. I am so sorry. Words cannot express how much I love you." I traced the lines of his face with my fingers and ran them through his hair. Wrapping my hand around his tattooed wrist I said, "Good-bye, Ian James. Rest in peace, son. We'll see you on the other side." The next day his body was cremated.

29

WHAT DO I DO NOW?

A week following Ian's funeral, I returned to the Vineyard Church, where I worked on the pastoral care team. When I opened the door, one of the pastors almost ran toward me, grabbing me like a rag doll. He cried as he held me. I had no tears, at least at that moment, and no words. Two other staff members saw me standing there limply, looking as awkward as I felt. When my colleague released me from his bear hug, he stepped back, gathered himself and in an almost breezy voice announced, "Well, brother, whew, you have been through it. So what's next?"

Completely taken aback, I almost burst into laughter and said, "Whew indeed! Glad we have that Follis kid's funeral behind us. Let's get back to ministry and growing this church." Instead, I shrugged my shoulders. "I have no idea. Time will tell." Giving him a nod, I turned, said "good morning" to the two staff members watching the ordeal and walked to my office, shutting the door behind me. For two hours I stared out the window before picking up my backpack and driving home.

———

The pastor who hugged me never brought up Ian's death again
—until six months later at our annual staff retreat. When we
arrived at a nearby state park, he came right up to me as we
unloaded and asked me to take a walk. I accepted his invitation, and within minutes we were heading down a trail. "I
think about Ian all the time," he said. "I would have talked to
you more but I just didn't know what to say. I pray for you
every day."

"Thank you for praying for me."

"I bet it's tough."

"You know it is. I don't really even know what I feel some
days. It depends on the day." Then he said the line I never liked
hearing. "*I just can't imagine what it must be like to lose a son.*"

"I can imagine it," I said. I decided to take a risk. "Since you
wonder about how I am doing emotionally I will just tell you
there are days I am really mad at God. Some days I let him have
it. It's no secret to him that I can swear." When he just stood
there looking at me blankly, I said, "Earlier today I said, 'God,
you are the one person who could have done something about
my son's death, but you sat on your fat butt and did nothing. I
hope you're happy!'"

Quickly reaching out and putting his hand on my shoulder,
he said, "Calm down, man. What are you saying? You need to
back off with that kind of talk about God and tell yourself the
truth." Half laughing, I said, "Ha! I didn't talk about God. I
talked to God. I figure God is a big boy and can stand on his
own feet whatever I say." He didn't back off. "Well, okay. I just
think you need to control your emotional responses a little
better."

He confused me. "Why are you so curious about my
emotions?"

"I care. That's why."

"Caring is good, but I have an idea for you. When you get back to your room, read Psalm 88. It's a Psalm of the sons of Korah. It will give you a good idea about my emotions—at least my emotions today." I did not tell him that Psalm 88 is the one Psalm that does not turn back from utter despair and ends: "You have taken my friend and neighbor—darkness is my closest friend."

It took all my self-control not to go at him hard. I wanted to say, "Don't bait me with your sincerity if you don't really want to know how I feel. You are an experienced pastor. You know better than to say something like that." Somehow I had the wherewithal to stay calm and say, "I'm ready to go back to the lodge." Our walk certainly had not gone the way I thought it would.

When we got back, he asked, "Did I offend you?" Shaking my head, I said, "Nope. You're fine." That was a response straight from the *Land of Numb*, but I didn't care. He never brought up reading Psalm 88, never again asked me how I was doing, and never again mentioned anything about Ian. A year later he moved away, and we never talked again.

30

THE THIEF COMES ONLY TO STEAL AND KILL AND DESTROY

On a dark February night, several months after Ian's death, Jennifer and I sat alone in our family room. Except for the lamp on the end table, the house was dark. We each curled up under separate blankets, sipping tea. Jennifer graded papers while I leafed through a dozen books on grief. Jennifer broke the silence. "I have a question for you."

"What is it?"

"Are we going to let the evil one get us?"

Her question startled me. I answered with the first thing that came to mind—"No, I'm not going to let that happen. We're together. That's settled; I'm not going anywhere."

"Me neither," she said. Holding a stack of papers in her lap, she paused and said, "We really have to stay together and be present if we're going to make it through this." I moved from my chair to the couch, where we wrapped our arms around each other. I could feel Jennifer's diaphragm expand and relax. I said again, "I'm not going anywhere."

"I didn't think so," she said, squeezing me tight. "Me neither."

Jennifer's question—"Are we going to let the evil one get us?"—came from the words of Jesus in John chapter 10: "The thief comes only to kill, steal, and destroy; I have come that they may have life, and have it to the full." An article I read after Ian died said that many marriages end after a couple loses a child. No question, it turns your world upside down. That evening we committed to stay the course. We didn't blame each other or ourselves for Ian's struggles. Our hearts broke for him, for ourselves, and for each other.

———

When you lose your 21-year-old son, the what-might-have-beens never leave. Through our grieving, Jennifer and I have gone on to live fulfilling lives, but the what-might-have-beens haven't left. Frankly, I wouldn't want them to. When his school friends married, we wondered what sort of family Ian might have created. When Ian's childhood friend named his first son "Ian" in his honor, we cried tears both of joy and regret. When we watch our granddaughters play, we muse about how much fun they could have had with their Uncle Ian.

On the third Sunday of Advent in 2022, the Anglican rector preached on joy. He is a young man the same age Ian would have been had he lived. A father-son duo leads our neighborhood Anglican church, the father serving as assistant under the son. They were both seated on the podium. It was fun to watch the father beam while his son delivered the Advent sermon. Then a pang of grief struck me. I thought, "That could be Ian and me up there." Grief is unpredictable, even after 15 years. It is always ready to return.

Yet grief fits the pre-Christmas theme, as Advent is a season for longing. The yearning is for both the coming of the Christ Child and for the day when history is consummated and

Jesus returns as King of Kings and Lord of Lords. That longing creates tension, which, of course, is a central point of Advent. As the book of Revelation ends, Jesus says, *Yes, I am coming soon.* St. John, the writer of Revelation, responds: *Come, Lord Jesus.* The tension is obvious—Jesus saying he will return soon and the writer John saying, "Don't delay. We're ready." *Come, Lord Jesus* is the most appropriate Advent response to the cries and longings of the faithful. Looking at the son and father in their Advent vestments, I turned my palms upward and accepted the longing, the mystery, the tension of Advent.

———

With Ian's death, I experienced sorrow unlike any other. People have asked me if the first year following his death was the hardest. "Yes," I say, smiling. "And the second, and the third." Grief is not linear. You can't put a timeline on grief. There is a time for everything—the intense mourning in the first year and the times when grief still catches you off guard in the grocery store. If the question is—as one pastor impertinently asked me—"Is your life finally getting back to normal?" the answer is "No." It is the wrong question. Jennifer and I have a new normal. There is no going back to normal when your child precedes you in death.

No family on earth is immune to losing children. Back when I was a college student I often drove past the exit for Abilene on my drive from Colby to Manhattan. Abilene is where President Dwight Eisenhower spent his boyhood and where he is buried. The first son of Mamie and Dwight Eisenhower was Doud Dwight, born in 1917. The boy died of scarlet fever on Jan. 2, 1921. President George H. and Barbara Bush lost their daughter Robin in 1953 to leukemia. Robin was 3 years old. The Eisenhowers almost never again mentioned their son —even to each other. The Bushes, however, talked about their daughter and liked it when people mentioned Robin's name. No two families handle their grief the same.

Back when our children were little, Jennifer and I became fast friends with Ron and Carolyn Butler—long-time missionaries in Africa. Ron died in 2010 in Cape Town. Carolyn, now in her mid-80s, still lives there but has lost not only her husband but all three of her children. Son Jeff was shot and killed in Kenya at 27 while working as a relief pilot. Son Greg and daughter Suellen both died of cancer at ages 58 and 59. Suellen and I were campus ministry colleagues at Illinois. While living in Central Africa, Carolyn had a good friend named Sikolastiki. Carolyn has written that during the years she knew Sikolastiki, she watched with her over the deaths of Sikolastiki's five children. Carolyn wrote, "An equanimity and calm acceptance bore her through her profound grief because God had revealed to her as a young bride that she would have five healthy children, but also that all her children would die before she did. Nothing I saw in her actions or heard in her words ever expressed anything but acceptance of this revelation and its fulfilment in her life."

Though we'd rather not have to, sooner or later all of us have to identify with the words of Job: "The Lord gave, and the Lord has taken away; blessed be the name of the Lord." Job 1:21 English Standard Version

———

Integrating my emotional and spiritual life requires consciously and constantly welcoming grief, whatever kind of grief it is. Though I don't tell anybody how to grieve, people often were willing, especially in the first year or two, to try to explain my grief for me. After Ian died, I got a handwritten four-page letter from an old campus ministry friend, a letter full of Bible verses, commentary and suggestions. It looked like he had worked plenty hard on it. He said it was all "intended for my comfort." The letter concluded with the story of his aunt recently burying her golden retriever, her constant companion for 15 years. "I have an idea of how you might be feeling," he wrote. "When I saw what my aunt went through when her beloved dog died, my heart went out to her. Fortunately, she made it through. In a few months, I pray that you will find you are able to move on even though, of course, you'll never forget your son."

I laughed, swore and tore the letter into little pieces and dropped them in the basket. I said out loud, "Please don't do that to anybody else ever again—comparing a dog's death to a child's death. Come on, man. You know better than that." The last thing I needed was some cheap talk about how spiffy it was that in a few months I would be able to move on or some pablum about how God needed another angel, whatever that means. "What's God's problem?" I thought the first time someone told me that. "Doesn't he have enough angels?"

I have learned that grief is grief. We all grieve differently. My grief over losing a son is mine. The grief experienced by the woman losing her dog is hers. The death of a long-time pet can be a huge loss. I live near a veterinarian who gets deeply emotional when he talks about having to euthanize animals. The best any of us can do is express love, empathy and kindness for all kinds of losses people experience—without feeling any need to compare our grief to theirs. That even includes me comparing my grief to Jennifer's. We grieve differently. After Ian died, people often asked me how Jennifer was doing. I always responded, "Why don't you ask her? She'd be glad to hear from you."

I try to say only a few phrases to grieving people: I am sorry; I can only imagine; I love you. Those are appropriate words about the griefs of each day and there are plenty of them. Jesus said each day has enough trouble of its own. Indeed it does. That's why asking someone "What was the best part of your day?" and "What was the hardest part of your day?" both are quite appropriate, as you give someone the chance to express their deepest positive and painful emotions. Feelings are feelings, and you just can't tell someone how they should feel. The responses you give to someone who expresses their grief of losing a loved one are similar to the ones you can use for any kind of grief. "I am so sorry. That sounds so hard. I so wish it were different for you. I love you." In short, that is grieving with those who grieve, and that is always the right thing to do.

If someone says their grief is not as bad as mine, it mini- mizes their grief. I try neither to maximize my grief, believing or saying it is the worst grief ever, nor to minimize it by stating that my sorrow is not as bad as someone else's. That's just not how grief works. Each grief is enough, and too much. One day I was talking with my neighbor Amy about her daughter who was soon going off to kindergarten. Amy started crying, saying, "I'm really going to miss her getting all tangled up in my legs while I cook. She is so looking forward to being in school like her older sisters, but I'm already missing her." Standing in the yard I said, "Amy, I can only imagine. It sounds hard. Jennifer and I sure enjoy having you as neighbors. We love watching you with your kids." Giving me a hug, she said, "Thanks, Don. I needed to hear that."

Over and over my heart is warmed by Jesus' words: *Blessed are those who mourn, for they will be comforted.* I feel certain that the words *I'm so sorry* never were far from his lips. They aren't far from mine either. Saying, *I am so sorry* sure beats crossing my arms and saying: "Well, it's just one of those things. There's a reason for everything. Who knows, God might have just needed another little angel. Give it time. You'll be *Just Fine* in no time."

31
RISKING THE UNIMAGINABLE

The Sunday after Jennifer and I had our heart-to-heart about staying the course in our marriage, a lay leader of the church came up to me while I was standing in the lobby greeting people. Though I hadn't spoken with this man since Ian died, that Sunday he walked straight up to me. He put his hands on top of my shoulders and looked straight into my eyes. "Don, I want you to know that I cannot imagine losing my son," he said, not mincing words. "I only have one son. I cannot imagine losing him." Shaking his head, he repeated himself, "I just cannot imagine losing him."

By the gentle, sincere tone of his voice and the way he held my shoulders, I knew he felt awful for me. But even if unwittingly, he had said the words I found the least comforting. Without hesitation, I responded, "You ought to try to imagine it." My words stopped him cold. As soon as I said them, he dropped his hands from my shoulders. "Yeah, I guess so. I haven't thought about it that way."

"You have just one son," I said. "He's a wonderful boy. I know you couldn't be prouder. Ian was my only son, too."

"Of course," he said. Giving me a hug, he said with utter sincerity, "I'm praying for you."

———

I am so thankful that before Ian died, Jennifer and I embraced and pushed in on the connection between emotional and spiritual health. Peter Scazzero's book had gotten me headed in the right direction, and I wasn't turning back. Following Ian's death, I was so committed to helping people connect their emotional and spiritual lives—pastors in particular—that I left my full-time pastor position at the Vineyard Church in Urbana and set up a not-for-profit organization to counsel, coach, and mentor pastors.

One phrase I have said hundreds of times as I meet with pastors is "I can only imagine." Of course, there are many things I really cannot imagine, and I know that. A person who never has lost a son truly cannot imagine it. Certainly not in the way that I can. So why should they even try? I do it because it forces me to hang between two worlds—mine and the pastor I counsel. Once I enter another person's world, I spend 90 percent of my time listening and asking questions. "What is the hardest part?" "What is the saddest part?" "What makes you happy? "What are your options?" "What do you think God wants you to do?" What's the real problem?" "What's really at stake?" "What is this costing you?" "What is this doing to those who also are affected by the decision?" "What's next?"

When a pastor says to me, "You listen well," or "You are easy for me to talk with," I take that as high praise. I never could listen well without being willing to hang between two worlds.

———

Eventually, Jennifer and I began leading two-day seminars for clergy couples on how to cultivate emotionally healthy marriages. In our seminars we asked lots of *what* questions. The first session we always warmed them up with an exercise asking them what they are feeling that very night. "What makes you glad, sad and mad?" The rhymes are not original with us. Counselors tell us that everyone, every day, feels both painful and positive emotions at the same time. It is true in every marriage, too. It is part of being human. People can feel glad, sad and mad all at the same time, sometimes about the same issues.

———

Learning from the Scazzeros, Jennifer and I started playing a game that we took right into our seminars. The first person asks, "What are you feeling right now?" The second person answers with either a painful or a positive emotion. The first person then asks, "When do you first remember feeling that emotion?" One day when Jennifer asked me how I was feeling, I answered, "Embarrassed." Earlier that day I was with a group of pastors and thought I had said too much. Afterward I felt embarrassed. Then came Jennifer's second question. "When is the earliest time in your life when you felt embarrassed?" I knew immediately. It was when I was in the fourth grade and the teacher accused me of making fun of a boy who was a poor reader. I felt horribly embarrassed because she scolded me in front of the whole class in a loud voice I never before had heard from her.

The game helps us quickly discover that the emotion we feel at any given moment is likely an emotion we have felt before. A 9-year-old doesn't have the language an older person has to describe emotions. But when I recalled the first time I ever felt embarrassed, the feeling was the same as it was when I thought I had said too much at that pastor's meeting. It's much easier for Jennifer to feel compassion for her tired husband when she hears the hurts shared by that lovable little redhead, Donny Follis.

———

Nowadays, I spend some time out on the streets among the homeless of Phoenix, listening to their stories, asking *what* questions and imagining what it is like to live on the streets of this city of five million people. What if I were the one without an address and without all my teeth? I put myself in the same physical location where that homeless person is because there is something critical about being in the immediate vicinity of another person's world. The closer I get to that world, the better I can try to imagine what it's like.

The other day I met a man in his mid-60s—a guy about my age. He said someone had stolen his backpack while he was taking a nap in a park. The backpack had his identification papers. He was distraught, and I tried to imagine having no identification papers. While a social worker and I spent a couple of hours helping him get a new ID, he began telling me about his favorite John Steinbeck and Flannery O'Connor books. I was surprised. He was both well-spoken and well-read. My heart went out to him as I tried to imagine being in his shoes—worn-out sneakers without any laces. He told me he had grown up in Iowa on a dairy farm, earned a teaching degree at Drake University in Des Moines, and taught high school English for 15 years in southern Iowa.

"What happened?" I asked.

"My marriage fell apart. Then I followed a woman out here

and that fell apart. Suddenly, I was living on the streets. It can happen faster than you think."

"I can only imagine. I am so sorry," I said.

"Yeah, me too. You know, I discovered that there is a fine line between making it and being on the street. And well—look at me now—I have no address. It's sure not how I want to end my days."

"Children?"

"Oh yeah," he said. "Three. They are all back in Iowa. Two will speak with me; one won't."

"Sounds really hard."

"Oh man. I miss them all every day. I've missed so many years. Lots of regret." He teared up but then quickly changed the subject and began telling me jokes. The jokes made him smile and me laugh. "Where did you get that good-looking smile?" I asked.

"Well, they say I got it from my mom, but I think I got it from my dad."

"I like it, wherever you got it. Keep smiling."

He thanked us for helping him get a new ID card. "I appreciate it. And by the way, I need a new hip, too. I am working on that next." Looking into his blue eyes, I tried to imagine a little boy growing up in Iowa. This 65-year-old man on the streets of Phoenix who needed a haircut, a shower, clean clothes, a good pair of shoes, and a new hip was once some Iowa mother's baby boy. Clearly limping, he winced as he walked over to me and hugged me. "I love you, man. Thanks again." Sometimes when you allow yourself to keep saying *I can only imagine*—hanging between your world and the world of someone else—you just might hear from the least likely person, "I love you, man."

32
JOY BEYOND THE WALLS

At the all-staff Christmas party a month after Ian's funeral, I laughed for the first time since Ian died. When the invitation to the party came, Jennifer and I thought about not going but decided we may as well be with people instead of sitting home alone. An ice-breaker started the evening as the 75 guests were instructed to grab two name tags and a marker. On one we wrote our name; on the other we wrote an emotion we were feeling during the Christmas season. The hostess said, "You guys, I love doing this. This is going to be so much fun. Christmas is my passion."

The emotion that popped into my head was "I wish I had stayed home." But I played along, picked up a Sharpie, wrote *Peace,* and stuck the tag on my sweater. The couple across from Jennifer and me wrote *Joy* and *Goodwill* on their tags. When I stood up to walk around the room and greet others, Jennifer tapped me on the shoulder. She pointed to the tag on her red sweater. The Christmas emotion she had written was *Bereaved.* Under *Bereaved* she had drawn a Santa face and a Christmas tree. I burst out laughing. Everyone in the room turned toward us. The senior pastor said, "Hey, you two. You're having way too much fun. Our Christmas party barely has started." No one saw the word *Bereaved* but me. Quickly pulling the name tag off her sweater, Jennifer replaced it with another one: *Hope*. The *Bereaved* nametag was perfect. In the context of the all-staff Christmas party—especially with the added Santa Claus face and Christmas tree—it did exactly what Jennifer intended, it made me laugh. She had not lost her wit. In our deep sorrow, we discovered that grief and joy always live together. Life is not a series of battles followed by a bucket full of blessings. Usually blessings and sorrows come intertwined.

Not long after that Christmas party I saw a 3X5 notecard lying on a table in a coffee shop with these words attributed to writer J.R.R. Tolkien: "We await a final Advent where we will experience joy beyond the walls of this world—poignant as grief." Though nothing had ever pierced my soul like the death of Ian, the good book says there is a better day coming—a day when history ends, the trumpet sounds, Jesus descends in the clouds as King of Kings and Lord of Lords and time will be no more. One day, time as we know it will conclude. There will indeed be joy beyond the walls of this world. The Apostle Paul said it like this, "What no eye has seen, what no ear has heard, and what no human mind has conceived—the things God has prepared for those who love him." (I Corinthians 2:9) I got my own notecard and copied the words ascribed to Tolkien, underlining the words joy beyond the walls of this world. For 15 years I have kept that notecard in the pocket of my journal. On the back, I wrote the words of the hymn *When I Survey the Wondrous Cross* by Isaac Watts. "See by his head, his hands, his feet; sorrow and love flow mingled down." Until this world ends, joy and grief are companions.

33

WEEPING IN KUNMING

J ennifer, Maddie and I decided to get away the first Christmas after Ian died. We didn't want to be home alone or to cast a shadow on anyone else's Christmas table. So we spent the week of Christmas in Cozumel, Mexico. Mostly I sat on the beach, stared at the water, and pondered the pain in the world while I read Os Guinness' *Unspeakable—Facing Up to the Challenge of Evil.*

A few months later I traveled to China for 14 days with a team from church. Jennifer stayed home in Illinois by herself, teaching her classes. She told me she was glad to be alone so she could sit and cry every night without having to put on a brave face for anyone. As we flew over the North Pole, I looked out the window into the seeming nothingness below and fantasized that Ian was sitting beside me, and that we were off on a grand adventure, hoping we could find a painting or a piece of pottery we could bring back home. In Kunming, a city of 12 million in western China, reality hit me right between the eyes and I saw something almost every day that fed my grief. At that point, it didn't take much. The first day it was a man screaming at a policeman. I had no idea what was going on, but both the man and the policeman were yelling. As we drove through a small village a couple of days later, I saw a man and woman fighting in full view of others. The woman's face was just inches from the man's. When she struck the air with her index finger, he turned away dismissively, incensing the woman even more. Turning to our translator, I said, "Roll down the window and tell them to stop screaming at each other." She just smiled and shrugged her shoulders. When we turned the corner, suddenly we were upon a funeral procession. Our translator pointed out two grieving women. A man held the arm of each woman, pulling them along. Seeing my demeanor change as I watched the procession, one of my team members asked, "Are you okay?"

"Nope," I said.

One morning at 6 o'clock, I left our hotel to take a walk. Within a block I was at Kunming's main intersection. Already thousands of people were on the streets—cars, bicycles, buses and people walking and running in every direction. In the middle of hundreds of people I shouted into the air. "Where in the world are all you people going?" Just then a van pulled alongside the curb. Two men jumped out, spread a blanket on the sidewalk and sat three metal cups on the edges of the blanket. Three disabled passengers were lifted out one by one and laid on the blanket. The two men jumped back into their van and drove off, leaving the three people there by themselves. Only one of the three could sit up, and he stared with an empty expression at the hordes of people rushing by. A few people put coins in the cups. As a traffic cop blew her whistle, I turned and walked back to the hotel. I shouted up to the sky, "What in the Sam Hill is going on down here anyway?" There was no answer.

34

A SUNDAY MORNING
FUNERAL DIRGE

Often with grief, we just don't know how we will react when it hits. And that makes some of us avoid it. One pastor I counseled said, "If I allowed myself to feel what some of my church members are feeling, I might start crying right in the pulpit while I preach."

"What would be wrong with that?" I asked. "Yes, that might happen. It might be the best thing that ever happened to you." He gave me a confused look and changed the subject.

A different pastor who had reached out compassionately to me after my son died, called me a year later and asked me to preach as part of a series on lament and grief. Since Ian had died, I had neither preached nor spoken to any groups. "Call me back in two weeks," I said. "I'm going to have to give it more thought." Exactly two weeks later he called and said, "If you aren't ready, I totally understand. What do you think?"

"I'll do it," I said.

"Tell as much or as little of your story as you want. Preach whatever message God gives you." A day later I lost heart and nearly backed out. Finally, I settled on combining some Psalms of Lament with the story in Luke 7 where Jesus resurrected a young man—the only son of a widow—just minutes before the son's scheduled burial on the outskirts of the city of Nain. When the pastor introduced me, he said, "My friend Pastor Don Follis is here today to continue our series on understanding grief and loss. I am especially touched to have him with us. Many of you know him through his Sunday religion columns in the paper. What you may not know is that Don lost his son a year ago at just age 21. Understandably, this is a poignant assignment for Don. I am so thankful for his willingness to come. We are deeply honored to have him in our pulpit. Please join me in welcoming Pastor Don Follis." The audience clapped. I didn't think he was going to say all that in his introduction. I felt awkward.

I laid my notes on the lectern, took a big breath and said, "Hello, everyone. How are you doing?" I scanned the 150 parishioners. "I bet you're wondering how I'll do today. I am too. I might cry; I might not. I don't really know. You hang with me, and I'll hang with you. Sound fair?"

They nodded, and I said, "It's a pleasure to be with you." My preparation paid off, as I quickly found my rhythm and felt surprisingly comfortable, especially given the subject. When I told the Luke 7 story, I said, "When Jesus and his entourage unexpectedly encountered this funeral processional, his heart instantly went out to the boy's mother." The faithful were with me as I said, "Can you imagine the pain felt by this mother—a widow who now has lost her only son." You can sympathize, I told them, but people don't want pity during times like that. They want understanding. "I don't want people feeling sorry for me," I said. "I don't want them saying, "Poor guy, a good man like this does not deserve this.'"

Most people feel loved if they know people come alongside them as their equal, sharing the same ground in this broken world as they do. To be of comfort, we must try to enter another person's world, enabling us to "mourn with those who mourn," as the Apostle Paul says. I asked, "How can we go into all the world and make disciples if we aren't intentional about at least trying to enter the world—the space—other people occupy? And as we all know, another person's world is almost always messy, with few easy fixes. Right now, though, I invite you to enter another person's world—mine." At that point, I stopped talking. I did something I never had done before. Walking to the edge of the stage, I said, "I want you to close your eyes and use your imagination."

The room fell silent. After a few seconds, I prayed, "Father, Son and Holy Spirit, help us to mourn with those who mourn. And if you so desire, anoint our eyes, and the cheeks of our faces, with the gift of tears." Looking up, I continued, "For just a few seconds I want you to imagine losing a child—like the widow in our story in Luke 7, like me in losing my 21-year-old son, and like many of you who have lost some of your closest loved ones. Picture Jesus' heart going out to the widow who was just minutes from seeing her only son buried. Many of you have lost a son, a daughter, a grandchild, a parent, a sibling or a close friend. Put your hands out in front of you with your palms facing up as you engage your imagination."

My plan was to let them sit with their thoughts, remembering their losses or imagining what it might feel like to lose a child. But after five or six seconds of silence, a woman sitting in a pew near the front let out a soft cry. Then her cry grew louder, piercing the silence in the room. Suddenly from the other side of the aisle, another woman cried. Her cry was more of a deep sob. The two women were singing a funeral dirge the likes of which I never had heard. A man beside one of the women put his arm around her and gave her a Kleenex.

When the crying subsided, I dropped my arms and clasped

my hands in front of me. Every eye in the room was on me. You could have heard a pin drop. "Friends, that is what it is like to imagine how a person feels when they lose a child." While the congregants composed themselves, I continued. "There are times when our sobs are too deep for words. We can only turn toward Jesus, who said, 'Blessed are those who mourn, for they will be comforted.' He gives us sighs too deep for words. Those laments are his Holy Spirit, ministering to us."

After the service, I stood in the foyer and greeted people. One woman hung back until everyone had left. Walking over to me, she said, "I was the first woman who cried out when you asked us to imagine what it is like to lose a child. A family in our neighborhood lost a 15-year-old daughter a few months ago. Until this morning, I've never imagined what it would be like had it been my daughter. I wouldn't let myself go there. My daughter is 15. But when you said to imagine losing a child, I decided to try it. As soon as I did, the dam broke and I wept. I hope I didn't make a scene. I'm sorry."

"Oh, please. Don't be sorry," I said, telling her that's how grief and loss feel, and sometimes how it sounds.

I told the woman, "Your response was normal. Actually, it was a beautiful lament. Thank you for trying to imagine—for being so present. God blesses those who mourn. Being able to mourn like that is real gift." She started to cry again. She grabbed my hand for a few seconds, composed herself, and left the building in silence.

———

Along about Wednesday of the following week, I received a note in the mail from a man who had been in that service.

I have spent most of life telling people, "I just can't imagine." Truth is, imagining what people are going through scares me, so I have pushed those thoughts and feelings far away. Last Sunday when you preached I saw how important it is to try to imagine how people feel, although in some ways we really can't. Still, it is important to try. You said love is stronger than death, and you are right. Others need our love more than anything. You prayed for some of us to get the gift of tears. That is not one I ever imaged getting, but the last two days I have cried like a baby about all the pain in the world. I never have been much of a crier, but now I am imagining that Jesus often must have freely wept because he could truly imagine the pain people felt.

35
SADNESS IN TENNESSEE

Two years after Ian died, I was invited to attend a three-day retreat near Knoxville, Tennessee, along with a dozen pastors and missionaries who had all lost a family member—most a son or daughter. For three days, I gathered with people I never had met before. We told our stories, grieved our losses and talked about what it meant to move forward. On the final day, we released our loved ones to the care and trust of the Lord by writing good-bye notes, attaching them to helium balloons and watching them rise high into the sky over the Tennessee River. Before the retreat, we were given detailed instructions about how to tell our story. "Preparing this should take you a couple of hours," they read. "The clearer and more honest you are, the more powerful it will be for you, and all those in attendance who are grieving. You each have 20 minutes to share your story. Be of good courage. I am praying for you."

The first morning we all sat in a big circle in overstuffed lounge chairs. On a small table in the middle was a large white candle. Before each person shared, the leader—a pastor who had lost a grandson—moved the table and candle in front of the next person slated to speak. The idea with the candle was to create a sacred space for each person. There were a half dozen boxes of tissues placed throughout the room. One specific ground rule in telling our stories the first day was that no one could touch another person while they shared—not even giving them a hug—even if they wept and had a hard time speaking. We hugged each other plenty the second and third days. But the first day was designed for each of us to sit with our own grief as we told our story. I had never done this in a group of people. Though we refrained from touching each other that first day, we did empty the boxes of tissues.

———

One woman talked about losing her husband. He was the senior pastor in the same church for 25 years. A pastor couple told about the death of their 18-year-old son who drowned trying to help a friend whose canoe capsized. A missionary couple wept as they spoke about losing their daughter, an only child, to brain cancer when she was not yet 30. I talked about losing Ian when he was just 21. And so it went, as person after person shared, with the white candle glowing directly in front of them. Finally it was time for a 65-year-old pastor to share his story. He looked at the burning candle in front of him but said nothing. Tears rolled down his cheeks as we all waited in silence for more than a minute, and then two minutes. His wife sat to his left. I wondered how long the leader would wait before finally intervening. We all waited, barely moving. Silently, I prayed for him, asking God to give him courage to speak.

"I don't think I can do it," he said, scarcely able to say even that. Then, haltingly, he began telling of losing his granddaughter a year ago. She had spent Friday night with Grandpa and Grandma. On Saturday morning they were having so much fun playing a game, he called her parents and asked if they could have a little more time. He broke into sobs, while the rest of us sat there, holding space for this heartbroken man. Regaining his composure, he continued, saying that when he and his wife drove his granddaughter home, a car ran a stop sign and T-boned their van on the side where his grand-daughter sat, securely buckled into her seat. She was killed instantly, less than a mile from his daughter's house. "I never will forgive myself," he said, holding one of the white tissues over his face and blowing his nose. For another minute he stared impassively at the candle. We all sat motionless, feeling his deep sorrow and pain, and pondering our own. He finally looked up at the group and said, "That's all."

PART SIX
TOTALLY PRESENT

On this side of having a better connection between my emotional and spiritual health, I find four truths keep reminding me to stay connected:

- A willingness to show up.
- Some things remain unfinished.
- It is appointed once for all humans to die.
- Integrating our emotional and spiritual lives is a lifelong quest.

36
A WILLINGNESS TO SHOW UP

In 2006 I made the sign of the cross over a newborn baby minutes before he died. I had befriended a young man at the Vineyard Church where I served on the staff. After services one Sunday, he approached me and asked if we could speak privately. Pulling me to the far side of a hallway where no one could hear us, he told me that a few days earlier he and his pregnant wife were told their child had a condition that would cause the baby to die within an hour or two of being born. Placing my hand on his shoulder I said, "Oh I am so sorry." Looking down at the floor, he stood silently before finally speaking in a voice I could barely hear. "When the baby arrives, will you come to the hospital and administer last rites?" No one had ever asked me to do that before. We didn't have that ceremony in the Vineyard or the Protestant church in which I was raised. For several seconds I was uncertain of how to respond, but when I saw his sincerity, I said, "Of course. I'd be honored."

He added, "After he dies, will you officiate at the funeral and burial?"

"Absolutely."

When I got home, I told Jennifer that I'd just been asked to give last rites for a baby who had not yet been born. She asked, "Do you even know how to do that?"

"I'll figure it out." After I researched it, I realized that Catholics don't do last rites for babies. The Catholic Church does offer parents in situations like these "The Rite of Final Commendation for an Infant," where a priest offers a short time of prayer to give the parents comfort and to commend and offer the infant to God. I decided that is what I would do. Just weeks before the baby was born, the soon-to-be father approached me again and said, "The baby's name is Zachary."

"That's a good name."

"When Zachary is born, I will call you. I have no idea what time of day that will be."

"Don't worry about that." At 11:45 p.m. on October 26, I was asleep when the phone rang. "Zachary is about to be born," was all the man said.

"I'll be right over." When I arrived at the hospital, a nurse directed me to sit in the waiting room. The baby would come any minute. A half hour later the physician who delivered Zachary came out of the room, shut the door, and motioned to me. He looked exhausted. When I walked over to him, he said, "The baby is still alive. You can go in."

Holding my Bible in one hand, I pushed the door open with the other and stepped into the room. There was little Zachary wrapped in a white blanket, snuggled in the crook of his mother's arm. Even when I walked to the side of the bed I could barely see him. I merely nodded to the parents, saying no words. A young blonde-haired nurse standing next to the hospital bed spoke, quietly saying, "I need to stay in the room. They said you were coming. I am a Mennonite." The new father nodded and said, "We're ready." Just as I had done hundreds of times, but never before in a hospital room with a baby not expected to live very long, I made the sign of the cross on myself and said, "In the name of the Father and the Son, and the Holy Spirit," adding, "Lord have mercy. Christ have mercy. Lord have mercy." Looking at the father, the mother, the nurse, and baby Zachary, I said, "Zachary, welcome to this world. What a gift you are to your father and to your mother." Zachary's eyes were closed and his nose was sunken into his face, but his skin was pink and his lips moved back and forth. The father and the mother stroked his head, repeating, "You are so beautiful, Zachary."

When my gaze met the nurse's eyes, I knew we were on sacred ground. Turning to Psalm 139 I paraphrased several verses, saying, "Zachary, God created your inmost being. He knit you together in your mother's womb. We praise God because you are fearfully and wonderfully made. Your frame was not hidden from God when you were made in your mother's womb. God's eyes saw your unformed body, and He sees you now. All the minutes ordained for you were written in God's book before any of them came to be." After the verses, the nurse stepped to the bed and put her stethoscope on baby Zachary's heart, holding it there for 30 seconds. "He is alive," she whispered. She nodded at me and I continued, reading Psalm 23 and saying, "Zachary, you are a deeply loved baby boy. Thank you for blessing us with your presence tonight. As our Lord Jesus committed his spirit to his Father, Zachary, we commit your spirit to the Father, the giver of life. You will live in his presence forever and ever."

Placing my thumb between my index and middle fingers on my right hand, I reached across the bed toward the baby. Making the sign of the cross 6 inches above Zachary's head, I said, "In the name of the Father, and the Son and the Holy

Spirit. The Lord gives and the Lord takes away. Blessed be the name of the Lord." The clock on the wall said 1:30 a.m. Looking at Zachary's father, mother, and the Mennonite nurse, I said, "If you wish, please join me in praying the Lord's prayer:

> *Our Father, who art in heaven, hallowed be thy name;*
> *Thy kingdom come, thy will be done,*
> *On earth, as it is in heaven.*
> *Give us this day our daily bread,*
> *Forgive us our trespasses, as we forgive those who trespass against us.*
> *Lead us not into temptation, but deliver us from evil.*
> *For thine is the kingdom, and the power, and the glory forever and ever.*
> *Amen.*

Taking three steps back, I leaned against the wall and watched the night unfold. The father nodded toward me and mouthed the words, "Thank you." The couple continued stroking Zachary's head, telling him how much they loved him. At 2:15 a.m., Zachary's lips quit moving. The nurse placed her stethoscope on his chest. This time she listened for an entire minute. No one moved. Draping her stethoscope over her neck, the nurse looked at the parents and moved her head from side to side. Zachary was gone.

I stood frozen to the wall, making myself as inconspicuous as possible. With baby Zachary still in the crux of her arm, the mother repeatedly kissed him, showing him to friends who had just arrived. "Isn't he just the most beautiful baby?" she said.

Finally excusing myself, I drove home. It was 4 a.m. when I slipped back into my bed.

"Is he gone?" Jennifer asked.

"He's gone." I was wide awake. At 4:30, I got up and made coffee. Sitting in my favorite chair, I held a mug of coffee in my lap and pondered the events of the night.

———

The next two days were a blur as I met with the family, planned the funeral and graveside services and wrote a sermon for baby Zachary. The morning of the funeral, a white casket barely larger than a shoe box sat in front of the lectern in the funeral home. Zachary's short life was "like a blip on a computer screen," I said. "Just like all of our lives in view of eternity."

Zachary was buried in a part of the cemetery called Baby Land. Several markers were engraved with toy bears or lions. I led a prayer of commendation and invited people to pray the Lord's prayer, just as I had with the parents and the nurse that night in the hospital. After I dismissed everyone, a man caught up with me and said, "Thank you so much for your remarks today. They were very comforting." I drove 35 miles home and thought about how grieving was such a crucial part of Jesus' ministry. Even though the last two days had been exhausting, I had been present and not off somewhere in the *Land of Numb*. It was not easy. I realized that at the graveside service I had tacked onto the Lord's Prayer, the ending of the Pledge of Allegiance. "With liberty and justice for all. Amen." I hope I didn't offend the hearers.

37
SOME THINGS REMAIN UNFINISHED

On a warm November 12 morning, Jennifer and I were walking through an arts festival in Fountain Hills, Arizona, stopping at the artisans' booths near the big fountain. Vendors spread out their wares for blocks. November 12 is the date of Ian's death, a day that Jennifer and I recall fond memories, sometimes light a candle, but always give thanks for our son. We have chosen to seek joy and to live full lives because we think that's what Ian would have wanted us to do.

As Jennifer and I made our way through the art festival, we came to the booth of a young painter. Draped over the display table was a vinyl banner with the business name printed on it: *Ian Unfinished*. The name stung us. Of all the names to see on the anniversary of our son's death? *Ian Unfinished*? When our Ian died, he was an art student at Parkland College in Champaign. Dying at 21, he definitely was an *Ian Unfinished*. I met the owner, a man in his mid-30s.

"Hi. Are you Ian of *Ian Unfinished*?"

"Sure am."

"I like the name."

"Thanks. What do you like about it?"

His question stopped me. "Ah, I just like how it sounds." For a moment I thought of telling him that I had a son named Ian who was an art student, but then pulled back and let it pass. Jennifer walked up and joined the conversation. "I like the name of your business. It reminds me of a sad story. Can I tell you?" Her question surprised me, though the name of the business begged the telling. Standing in his booth, Ian said, "Ah, sure, I guess." Reading his hesitation, Jennifer backed off. "Well, let me tell you a happy story. I once knew an Ian who loved art, like you. Seeing your artwork reminds me of him and makes me think what you're doing is great. Keep it up."

Ian smiled and said, "Thanks."

"Have a good day, Ian," she said.

———

As we meandered through the booths that November morning, my phone rang. It was my friend Kyle, just calling to say he remembered it was the anniversary day of Ian's passing. Just a few years older than Ian, Kyle has called me on nearly every anniversary of Ian's death. Kyle and his wife, Ellen, were missionaries in Mexico when I was on the staff of the Vineyard Church. Six times I traveled to Mazatlán to see them. On one of my trips, Kyle and I took a long walk. After coming upon a cemetery, we meandered our way through the graves. Kyle stopped at the headstone of a teenager, a boy who had died at age 16. "It must be so hard for you to keep carrying on the way you do, after you and Jennifer lost Ian," Kyle said. "How do you do it?"

"One day at a time," I said.

Patting my shoulder, Kyle said, "I admire you for hanging in there. I know you don't have much choice. I love you."

38

IT IS APPOINTED ONCE FOR
ALL HUMANS TO DIE

The New York Times is known for its well-written obituaries. When I began reading them 30 years ago, I never imagined that one day I would have to write my own son's. Each day I read the obituaries from *The New York Times*, *The (Champaign-Urbana) News-Gazette* and *The Arizona Republic*. Every week in Phoenix, Maricopa County places a dozen or more death notices in the *Arizona Republic* of people whose bodies have not been claimed. Most are of people between the ages of 25 and 60. Some are named; some are not. Not long ago there were death notices of two newborn babies. Maricopa County was looking for information about them, too.

Each death notice says: *"If you have any information regarding this person, please call Maricopa County Indigent Decedent Services."* There is a number to call at the bottom of each notice. Out of curiosity, one day I called the number and asked how the process works. What I really wanted to know was how many cases are resolved. A woman was eager to chat.

"How many unsolved cases are you working on right now?" I asked.

"About 50," she said.

"Fifty?" I exclaimed. "That's a lot."

"Closer to 60, actually."

"I can only imagine. How do you do it?"

"Well, I figure everyone deserves to be claimed before they are laid to rest. I do my best to bring resolution to each case—however short or tragic their life may have been."

"My goodness. What a job you have have—an important job."

"I think so, too."

"What is a typical day? Or is there one?" I asked.

"Oh, sure. First we look at identification. Almost all those people whose death notices you see in the paper had some form of identification when they died, obviously, or they never would have made the paper. The county is looking for as much information as possible. Does the person have a history here in the Phoenix area? Do they have a family? Does anyone know them? Are there any phone numbers?"

"Do you get what you are looking for?" I asked.

"Sometimes yes, but often no. Just other day we got word that a fellow died on the streets here in Phoenix. Sadly, it happens frequently." The man had a wallet and ID. Inside his wallet was a phone number written on a piece of white paper. She called the number. "A man answered, and it turned out to be this man's brother. He thought his brother lived in Las Vegas, not Phoenix."

"Did he want to come and identify his brother's body?" I asked.

"No. He said we could cremate the body and bury the ashes. Actually, he was relieved. He assumed his brother had been dead for years."

"Where did you bury the ashes?"

"In White Tanks Cemetery, a Maricopa County owned

facility on the far west side of Phoenix. Hundreds of dear souls are buried there. And that's what we did with this man's ashes." She explained that a volunteer chaplain officiates while a few inmates volunteer as honorary pallbearers. Even in burying ashes, they recruit four to six pallbearers. In their prison garb, the pallbearers stand beside the chaplain, giving witness to the life and death of the deceased. They sing *Amazing Grace.*

Not long after that conversation, I drove to White Tanks Cemetery early one morning. When I arrived, there was a man in a khaki work uniform spraying the ground. A mask covered his face as he dragged a hose connected to a 200-gallon tank sitting on a flatbed truck. When I walked toward him, he shut off the sprayer, pulled down his mask and hollered, "Good morning."

"Good morning," I called back. "What are you spraying?"

"Pre-emergent weed killer. The county doesn't want anything growing out here in the cemetery."

Smiling, I said, "This cemetery is brought to you by the color tan."

"You got that right," he answered, pointing to his pants and shirt. "Just like my outfit." There were no trees; no grass; no flowers; no bushes; not even a cactus. But six inches above the ground are hundreds of metal discs the size of a coffee cup saucer. Names and dates are engraved on each marker.

As the man showed me around, he said he was 36 years old and nine months out of prison. His grandmother raised him but she died while he was in prison. Her death got his attention. "When I got out, I decided to live for her," he said. A landscape company gave him a chance. "I'm doing great so far," he said, wiping the sweat from his brow. "I got here at 5 this morning."

"You are the early bird."

"I like being out here early. It gives me time to think. It reminds me of where I could have ended up, especially after some of the choices I made. I got the chance that some of the people out here never got. I am one of the lucky ones."

When I started to say good-bye, he beckoned me walk with him to a nearby disc that read *Male—#164527*. There was no name and no dates—only the number tying it to the county coroner's office. Removing my cap, I bowed my head and paid my respects. Looking at the man dressed in tan I said, "Wow."

Shaking his head he said, "Yep, life can be really tough." We shook hands and I said, "I'm real proud of you, man. Stay the course. No turning back now."

"Thank you, sir. Thank you so much. You're right. No turning back now."

Walking past row after row of metal discs, I headed to my car, thinking of these words from the book of Ecclesiastes: *It is better to go to a house of mourning than to go to a house of feasting, for death is the destiny of everyone; the living should take this to heart.* Ecclesiastes 7:2

39
A LIFELONG QUEST

When I wasn't in my class on spiritual formation at Phoenix Seminary during my summer sabbatical in 2017, I mostly sat by the pool at my Scottsdale condo, reading books. I had 10 weeks to consider how solitude affects the inner life and wrote a 6-week course for pastors on how the inner life affects their emotional health. Every Friday morning I put my books aside and headed out on the streets with a team from Phoenix Rescue Mission. In a van called the Hope Coach, we drove to the different homeless camps scattered throughout Phoenix. To homeless folks trying to find respite from the desert heat, we gave out water, Popsicles, and supplies to make life a tad more bearable. One cloudless Friday the temperature rose to 105 by noon. When the temperature rises above 105, even the locals complain. At our first stop, I spent 30 minutes standing in the sun talking with a fellow named Dale, a shirtless 22-year-old man wearing long black Nike shorts and rubber sandals. A tattoo across the top of his chest read: *Sorry Mom.*

"What's your tattoo mean?" I asked.

"It has two meanings. It means I'm sorry for all the crappy decisions I have made in my 22 years of life and will probably continue to make. And it means I'm sorry that Mom and I are both meth addicts. She's out here on the streets somewhere. Occasionally, I see her. We have good talks. She's a good mom and a good person. She just can't get her life together. I guess I can't either. I love her, even though I mostly lived with my grandma while I was growing up."

Our team leader told Dale how the Phoenix Rescue Mission offers a year-long program to help folks get back on track. I said, "It doesn't cost you anything. Why don't you come back to the mission with us today? You can try it out for a couple of days. We have room for you in the Hope Coach. You can take a shower. We can get you some clothes and some shoes. We'll get you something to eat. You can sleep in an air-conditioned dorm. You can stay there two days, sitting in on some of the lessons, to see if you want to commit to the program."

"Do they allow dogs?" Dale asked. "Because if they don't, I am not interested in knowing anything more. I don't go anywhere without my dog." A black Lab lay at Dale's feet. He let his dog drink from one of the plastic bottles of cold water I had given him and eat a cherry-flavored Popsicle.

"Sorry. Pets are not allowed."

"Like I said," Dale insisted. "I don't go anywhere without my dog, not even to try your program for a couple of days." And that was it. He grabbed the leash, and the black Lab jumped up ready to go. Dale accepted two more Popsicles and walked away with his dog, heading straight into the blazing sun.

Back at the mission headquarters that afternoon, minus a few hundred bottles of water and two hundred Popsicles, I saw a man sitting alone at one of the picnic tables under a huge fan.

"Hi. I'm Don."

"Call me Sunny Bear," he said. Turns out, Sunny Bear had

just arrived from the Zuni reservation in northwestern New Mexico.

"What brought you here?" I asked.

"I got kicked off the reservation."

"You got kicked off the reservation?"

"Yep, for doing bad things."

"Sounds tough. Sorry."

"It is. Sitting here is the last place in the world I want to be."

"Then why are you here?"

"It's where they dropped me off."

"So, are you Zuni?"

"No, Navajo. My girl is Zuni. I was on the Zuni reservation when I was arrested and removed. I deserved it."

"You deserved it?"

"For sure. I do crazy things, man, especially when I am drunk." When Sunny Bear learned that I am a pastor, he started calling me Rev. "Hey, Rev. Is it okay if I call you that?"

"Whatever you like."

"You like being a reverend?"

"Yeah, it's okay. It has its ups and downs."

"Like anything, huh?"

"Pretty much."

Sunny Bear told me about growing up in northern Arizona on the Navajo reservation and how he can speak the language. Until he was 17, Sunny Bear lived there. At age 10 or 11, he doesn't exactly remember, he was removed from his home and put into a church-based orphanage. "I hated it, but I guess there was one good thing."

"Tell me about one good thing about a place you hated," I said.

"Even though I fought everyone and broke every rule, I became a Christian when I was 12. Pretty cool, huh Rev?"

"Pretty cool, Sunny Bear."

"Rev, I accepted Jesus Christ as my Lord and Savior as a 12-year-old kid. I guess I'm still a Christian, even though I usually don't act like one."

"There are lots of ups and downs in life, Sunny Bear."

"That's the truth, Rev. I try to do the right thing. Well, some of the time." Looking straight at me, he asked, "Do you think I'm still a Christian, Rev?"

"I do, Sunny Bear. I sure do."

"The guy in charge of the orphanage told me he didn't think I was or I would quit making such terrible decisions that always seemed to hurt a lot of people. He might be right." Exhaling and shaking his head, he said, "Somewhere along the way I quit making good decisions."

"Sounds hard."

"Yeah, man. It's really hard—really, really hard—especially right now."

"I'm so sorry."

"Don't be sorry, Rev. It's not your problem. I made my choices. But even when I try to make good choices and do the right thing, they usually don't work out." Sunny Bear said he left the orphanage when he was 17. "That was 13 years ago. I think."

"What have you done in the last dozen years?"

"About half of it was in prison. A few part-time jobs. On and off the reservation a few times. That's about it."

"Wow. What do you want to do next?"

"No idea, Rev. Get out of here as soon as I can and get back with my woman. Although, after the last few days, she said she never wants to see me again."

"Sounds hard, Sunny Bear."

"Yeah, I suppose, but I'm not worried about it. I'll win her back. Deep down she loves me. Just not when I drink." Lifting up his right forearm, Sunny Bear showed me a tattoo of a woman with long black hair. Beads encircled her neck. To the side of her face written in cursive were the words *Savage Passion.*

"Is that your woman?"

"Yep. Beautiful, isn't she?"

"Sure is."

"She's the most beautiful Indian woman I have ever met, Rev." For the first time, Sunny Bear smiled. After a few more minutes of small talk, I stood and said, "Sunny Bear, I am really glad I met you. I need to roll. Keep your head up, pal."

"Yeah, Rev. I have to." As we shook hands I asked, "You got anything else for me, Sunny Bear?"

"Yeah I do, Rev. Will you pray for me? Pray that I will quit throwing my life away."

"May I pray for you before I leave?"

"I want you to." Sunny Bear stuck his right arm toward me. "Lay your hand right on her head, Rev." I placed my hand on Sunny Bear's right forearm. "God," I prayed, "Please help Sunny Bear quit throwing his life away and please bless this beautiful Indian woman. Amen."

"Thanks, Rev. Maybe I'll see you again, huh?"

"I'd like that, Sunny Bear."

"Me too, Rev."

———

Every week that summer, my class at Phoenix Seminary began with two students telling their stories, explaining how they came to study spiritual formation. As I had seen with Dale and his dog and then with Sunny Bear, everyone's story includes pain—usually a lot of pain. Most of the 15 students were under age 40. At 62, I was the oldest. Two had been divorced. One had lost a spouse. Another had a brother die at age 30. And of course I had lost my son. After Jennifer and I returned to Illinois, a pastor friend asked me to give him a one-sentence synopsis of my 10 weeks studying spiritual formation. "Let God take your pain and shape you into the person he wants you to be," I said.

"Sounds intense," he said.

———

After spending the day giving out water and Popsicles and talking with Dale and Sunny Bear, I pulled past Paradise Memorial Gardens on East Shea Boulevard in Scottsdale and into the parking lot of the condo we rented for the summer. With my car running and the air conditioner blowing cool air in my face, I prayed, "God, please help Dale and his dog and his Mom and Sunny Bear and his woman to quit throwing their lives away. Please keep them safe. And keep the students in my spiritual formation class safe, too." When I stepped into the condo, Jennifer kissed me, looked at me and asked, "Are you okay?"

"Yep, I'm okay. But I'm not *Just Fine*." Plopping down on the couch, I closed my eyes and said, "And Lord, help me not to lose hope."

EPILOGUE

Researching this book gave me reason to call my ex-wife. The day after we talked, I texted her, thanking her for the conversation and including a blessing to her and her husband. Her response back to me was gracious, and for that I am grateful.

When Jennifer and I pulled into Illinois in July 1978, 10 days after we were married, I thought we might stay two or three years, long enough for Jennifer to finish college. We stayed two or three years all right—43 to be exact! We became townies—raising our children, teaching Sunday School, volunteering in schools, coaching park district sports, serving in church leadership and making life-long friends. Jennifer had a long career teaching journalism at the university; I wrote hundreds of religion columns for the local paper. Our son is buried there. It is where our daughter was married. And it was there I quit being

Just Fine, where I faced my shame, and where I left the *Land of Numb.*

Finally, in July 2021, Jennifer and I did what we had seen people do for years in Champaign-Urbana. We loaded up and left town, traveling 1500 miles back to Phoenix. On our wedding day we pulled out of the *Valley of the Sun* in a baby-blue 1974 Ford LTD. With Jennifer snuggled next to me on the bench seat, we giggled all the way to Sedona, where we spent our first night. Moving back, we took a different route and exited I-40 at Holbrook. We then drove south 180 miles, descending 5,000 feet from the Mogollon Rim and down into the same valley we had left four decades earlier. As we drove into Phoenix in a 2019 Honda CRV, we looked at each other as if to say, "That went fast."

"How could it possibly have been 43 years?" I asked.

"One day at a time, honey," she said. "Welcome back."

ACKNOWLEDGMENTS

Thanks to all the people who've accompanied me on this journey. Thanks to Oakley Christian Church for paying my college tuition.

Thanks to Ruth Wegman for reading the first draft of this book and making excellent suggestions, including smiley faces. Ruth, you are a good editor, and a kind person.

Thanks to John Ciciora for giving the book a lovely cover.

And thanks especially to Jennifer Follis, who has lived this story with me. I promise I will quit saying every evening, "Could I tell you something else about my book?"

ABOUT THE AUTHOR

Don Follis directs Pastor-to-Pastor Initiatives, a ministry helping leaders connect their emotional and spiritual lives. Don spent 43 years working in Champaign-Urbana, Illinois, as both a campus minister and church pastor. Along the way, he wrote the Sunday religion column for *The News-Gazette*. Don and his wife, Jennifer, live in Tempe, Arizona. Continue the journey at donfollis.com.

STUDY QUESTIONS

1. Do you come from the *Land of Numb* where everyone is *Just Fine*? What was life like in the family and place where you were raised?
2. What were the main emotions in your family—both painful and positive?
3. In the *Land of Numb* where everyone is *Just Fine*, it was easy for Don to kick himself when things went wrong. When do you put on your kick-me sign? Can you take it off and tell yourself the truth?
4. What does it mean to be fully present? When is it easiest for you to notice that your emotional and spiritual lives are integrated?
5. In the story in Luke 7:35-50, Jesus lets himself feel the full weight of both painful and positive emotions at the dinner party to which he was invited. What painful and positive emotions can you find in this story?

6. What is the difference between saying, *I just can't imagine what you are feeling* and saying, *I can only imagine what this is like for you?*

7. How can you be true to yourself while also being fully connected to people by entering their world? Are you able to detach and allow space between yourself and another, even if the other person needs to be "rescued?"

8. The Apostle Paul writes in Romans 12, "Rejoice with those who rejoice and mourn with those who mourn." When have you done that?

9. After Jesus was baptized, God's voice boomed from heaven, saying, "This is my Son, whom I love; with him I am well pleased." Have you heard God say something like that to you? How is identity as a child of God foundational to a fully integrated emotional and spiritual life?

TELLING YOUR STORY

After I returned from the three-day session where 12 pastors and missionaries told their story of loss, I developed my own version of "Telling Your Story." The stories don't have to center on grief, although there usually is plenty of that in every life.

I focus on pastors, but any small group could do this. I begin by inviting four or five pastors to come to my house on a weekday morning to tell their stories and then eat lunch together. Most never have done anything like this. After people agree to come, I send specific instructions for preparing, similar to the ones I received before the Tennessee retreat on grieving our losses. Before they attend, I require they watch a TED Talk by Brené Brown on the power of vulnerability. Each pastor is given 22 minutes. Two weeks beforehand I send this email:

> "What is the main theme of your story? Think about what is at the heart of what you want to say. What is it, deep down, that you really want others to know about your story? This is not an autobiographical sketch. You do not have to say

anything you do not want to. But I want you to tell a true story, one centered on the main theme of your life. That's why it is important to carefully prepare. Outline your story and then write it out word for word. My story is nine pages, doubled spaced. Practice it and time yourself. When we begin, I will tell my story first—speaking, among other things, about my teenage marriage and divorce, about how I thought that would keep me from ever entering the ministry, about how my only son lost his battle with drugs, and about my life-long struggle with making clear, resolute decisions."

I feel it is only fair for the storytellers to know I am going to be vulnerable along with them. I follow up the first email with three or four other short, encouraging emails, thanking them in advance for their willingness to tell their story and saying how much I am looking forward to hearing it. When the day arrives, participants are excited and nervous, especially given how I built up the importance of being well prepared and vulnerable. Circling the chairs in my family room, I light a white candle, just as we had done in Tennessee. I go first, modeling how I hope the day will unfold. Before each pastor talks, I move the table and candle in front of him, and say, "Let's all quiet our hearts for a few seconds, breathing in and out." Turning to the next storyteller I say, "Whenever you are ready, please begin."

Given the high level of transparency and vulnerability shown by the speakers, often there are both tears and laughter. Almost every time at the lunch that follows, someone says, "I've never done that in my life. That was powerful." No cross-talk is allowed all morning. No, "Let's just stop and pray for Jim." No, "The Lord spoke to me clearly when you told your story. I'd like to share what he said." None of that. This is a time to listen to each other, holding the stories in our hearts, letting each story speak for itself. It is a morning for holding space for those who are courageous enough to be vulnerable and for imagining what it must be like to be in another person's shoes. Those who want to talk more set up times to get together privately.

After each story, we recite in unison from a card I give to each person.

Thank you so much for sharing your story with us this morning. We are honored. May God the Father, God the Son, and God the Holy Spirit bless you in your life and ministry. You are God's child whom he calls beloved. We will hold your story in our hearts.

RECOMMENDED READING

Bonhoeffer, Dietrich. *Letters and Papers From Prison.* Fortress Press, 2015. Among these powerful and touching letters and papers is Bonhoeffer's poem *Who Am I?* For me, no poem better addresses the struggle of our emotional and spiritual lives.

Boyd, Gregory A. *Present Perfect—Finding God in the Now.* Zondervan, 2010. Boyd's book called me over and over to be fully present.

Butler, Carolyn. *Under African Skies—Reflections for Advent and Christmas.* Lux Verbi.BM, 2008. These are my long-time missionary friend's inspirational devotions for Advent and the 12 Days of Christmas. Her writing is full of longing for Jesus' return. I have read them every year since Ian died.

Card, Michael. *A Sacred Sorrow—Reaching Out To God In The Lost Language of Lament.* NavPress, 2005. Card gives everyone permission to grieve. He argues that even at Sunday morning church there should be permission to cry and grieve. I couldn't agree more.

Groothuis, Douglas. *Walking Through Twilight: A Wife's Illness—A Philosopher's Lament.* InterVarsity Press, 2017. Groothuis is a philosophy professor at Denver Seminary. This is the moving story of his wife's dementia and death when she still was middle-aged. Groothuis offers no easy answers and shows how bewildered he felt as his wife's life ebbed away.

Guinness, Os. *The Call—Finding and Fulfilling The Central Purpose Of Your Life,* Word Publishing, 1998. This is a wonderful book on calling that I have read over and over. Guinness considers 25 angles of God's call. Solid emotional health is vital to get a true understanding God's call.

Guinness, Os. *Unspeakable—Facing Up to Evil in an Age of Genocide and Terror.* HarperSanFrancisco: A Division of HarperCollins Publishers, 2005. Guinness calls us to live an examined life. He says we must come to terms with our beliefs about evil if we are going to fight against it. Every life gets put to the test. This book forced me to think long and hard about what kind of faith I would have in light of my son's death.

Lederach, John Paul. *Reconcile—Conflict Transformation for Ordinary Christians.* Herald Press, 1999. Lederach has worked in 25 countries, helping groups face conflict. If I am going to be a man of peace, willing to speak the truth in love, I cannot do it from the *Land of Numb.* To resolve and transform conflicts with others, and even myself, I have to be willing to speak up, feel real emotion and face conflict, even if it means not being liked.

Lewis, C.S. *The Great Divorce.* Macmillan Publishing Co., 1946. This is Lewis' delightful story of a bus ride from hell to heaven. When I finally decided to leave the *Land of Numb*, this book helped.

Linn, Dennis. *Sleeping with Bread—Holding What Gives You Life*. Paulist Press, 1995. There are all kinds of books on the Daily Examen, but this is the first one I read and is a perfect little book to read if you want to introduce the Examen in your life. Practicing the Examen was a godsend in helping me get in touch with true emotions after Ian's death.

McQuiston II, John. *Always We Begin Again—The Benedictine Way of Living*. Morehouse Publishing, 1996. McQuiston rewrites The Benedictine Rule in modern language. It is full of beautiful reflections and prayers. Nearly every morning I pray part of Benedict's morning prayer: *Grace to us and peace. We do not know what this day will bring—life is the great enigma; life is the great good; we expect good from this day. At all times and at this time we participate in the great Mystery. We acknowledge our contingent nature. We humble ourselves before that which we do not understand. When we consider the vast reaches of the cosmos, the incomprehensible forces at work in the moment, the numberless stories of each life, the millions of forgotten ancestors who preceded us, the untold acts of kindness which occur each day. We humble ourselves.* (P. 73-74)

Scazzero, Peter. *The Emotionally Healthy Church—A Strategy for Discipleship that Actually Changes Lives*. Zondervan, 2003. This is the book that let me out of the *Land of Numb*. I've been using these principles for 20 years.

Scazzero, Peter. *Emotionally Healthy Spirituality*. Thomas Nelson, 2006. Here Scazzero pushes deeper, reflecting on integrating our emotional and spiritual lives. Excellent!

Sittser, Jerry. *A Grace Disguised—How The Soul Grows Through Loss*. Zondervan, 1995, 2004, 2021. This book was my refuge after Ian died. It is the story of the terrible accident that took the lives of Sittser's mother, his first wife and one of his daughters. Sittser himself survived the accident and this is his deep reflection on the meaning of that tragedy. I first read it 10 years before Ian's death and have read it three or four times since his passing. It's my go-to book on emotionally healthy grieving.

Wolterstorff, Nicholas. *Lament for a Son*. Eerdmans Publishing Co., 1987. Wolterstorff, a Yale Divinity School philosophy professor, reflects on the sudden death of his 25-year-old son in a mountain-climbing accident. He reflects on how the sting of losing a child never leaves you.

Made in the USA
Monee, IL
11 August 2023

40849810R00144